W9-AEV-482

Free Speech on Campus

Issues in Academic Ethics
Series Editor: Steven M. Cahn

Free Speech on Campus

Martin P. Golding

ROWMAN & LITTLEFIELD PUBLISHERS, INC.
Lanham • Boulder • New York • Oxford

ROWMAN & LITTLEFIELD PUBLISHERS, INC.

Published in the United States of America
by Rowman & Littlefield Publishers, Inc.
4720 Boston Way, Lanham, Maryland 20706
http://www.rowmanlittlefield.com

12 Hid's Copse Road
Cumnor Hill, Oxford OX2 9JJ, England

British Library Cataloging in Publication Information Available

Library of Congress Cataloging-in-Publication Data

Golding, Martin P. (Martin Philip), 1930-
    Free speech on campus / Martin P. Golding
        p.   cm.   —(Issues in academic ethics)
    Includes bibliographical references and index.
    ISBN 0-8476-8791-0 (alk. paper)—ISBN 0-8476-8792-9 (pbk. : alk. paper)
    1. Academic freedom—United States. 2. Freedom of speech—United States. 3. College
students—Civil rights—United States. 4. Education, Higher—Moral and ethical
aspects—United States. I. Title. II. Series.
LC72.2.G64 2000
378.1'012—dc21   99-049743

Printed in the United States of America

∞™ The paper used in this publication meets the minimum requirements of American
National Standard for Information Sciences—Permanence of Paper for Printed Library
Materials, ANSI/NISO Z.39.48–1992.

Contents

Contents

Preface

I was a student at the University of California at Los Angeles during the heyday of the "loyalty oath" controversy. The Cold War was at its beginnings, and the fidelity of some academics to the United States was questioned. Employees of the university, including faculty, were required to take an oath that they were not members of so-called subversive organizations. As far as I could tell, none of my teachers was a supporter of the Soviet Union or communism (well, maybe a few), but I knew some students who were. My own attitude toward communism, however, had been negative since my high school days. I had had a teacher who was a fellow traveler, if not a member of the Communist Party, and he often lectured us callow youth on the virtues of that system. He never converted anyone, and I developed an antipathy toward the Soviet system. (In other respects he was the best high school teacher I had.) So I might have been expected to be a supporter of the loyalty oath. But I was not.

It seemed to me then, as it seems to me now, that universities are hallowed ground, as it were: the free expression of ideas and opinions, and their critical examination, are central to the work of the university. This faith, I admit, was put into question during the student disruptions in 1968 at Columbia University, where I was then teaching. I was shocked by students who wanted to "bring the university to its knees" and who thought they could thereby force a radical transformation of society. I was even more shocked by their faculty supporters who were willing to foul their own nests and risk destroying the institution. Yet, though we now live in the wake of these events, I still retain a belief in campus free speech.

However, I am not a free speech "absolutist." Free speech is a value that must be weighed against other values and that could be overridden by them. There are circumstances in which the freedom of speech may be curtailed, but these circumstances are always special. Thus, to take an extreme case, an argument can be made that it is legitimate in today's Germany to curb the verbal activities of neo-Nazi organizations, given the special history of the country. (Currently,

vii

Hitler's *Mein Kampf* cannot be published there, though the Internet makes it fully available.) It may, however, be unwise to do so. Much depends on context.

On the other hand, though free speech is not an absolute value, it may have a special weight in certain circumstances. Any move to curtail it would then have a hard burden to overcome. This, I believe, is the case in universities.

This book is concerned with free speech on campus, but it is not about the First Amendment to the U.S. Constitution. It is, rather, a study in "institutional ethics." To be sure, public universities and colleges are bound by the First Amendment's guarantees of the freedom of speech, and perhaps private institutions are too, to some extent. There are, however, many excellent studies on the constitutional right of free speech. Instead, this book examines arguments, pro and con, concerning standards of discourse and expression that are particularly germane to the campus context, public or private, whether or not they are constitutionally enforceable. It will, nevertheless, be impossible to avoid some discussion of the First Amendment guarantees. Many of the arguments regarding campus discourse and expression turn on the question of how these guarantees are to be understood.

This book is also not a survey of the speech code literature. I take up what seem to me to be the best arguments for speech codes, try to present them sympathetically, and evaluate them. I come out, in the end, against speech codes. But this conclusion doesn't make me happy, for I think that it is not necessarily right to do something simply because it is legally or institutionally unpunishable: civility and concern for the feelings of others do not lose their importance whether or not there are speech codes. It also doesn't make me happy to support, as I do, the freedom of expression for the many silly and repellent theoretical ideas and opinions that the American campus is so full of today, though some might be excludable on academic grounds. As is emphasized throughout, the issue is not just the unitary one of whether there should be speech codes. There in fact is a complex of campus speech issues, connected with each other in greater or lesser degree.

We should not leave this preface without taking notice of what has been happening on campuses in recent years: an increase in the number of reported incidents of racial conflict; pressure for a more "multicultural" curriculum and revision of the "canon" (the fields, subjects, and books that hitherto have been standardly taught); affirmative action programs in admissions and faculty recruitment; regulations dealing with sexual harassment; regulations governing dating between students and between students and faculty (the Duke University law school has adopted regulations against dating between law students and faculty); "consciousness raising" sessions and sensitivity training, and so on. Around these various incidents, pressures, programs, regulations, and activities, there has grown up a veritable industry of administrators and "facilitators."

How are these phenomena connected to the campus speech issue? Does a stand on the speech question commit one to a particular stand vis-à-vis any one or other of these matters? For instance, does a pro-regulation stand commit one to a program of affirmative action or multicultural education? The rhetoric surrounding the free speech issue, from parties on both sides of the debate, the pro-regulators and the anti-regulators, often suggests that there may be a connection. But a connection of what sort? Is there some conceptual link that ties them together? Do they flow together from some social ideology or agenda? Or is it merely accidental that proponents and opponents of speech regulation also tend to take contrary stances on these other phenomena?

These are difficult questions, and we cannot pretend to answer them in this book. Each side to the debate tends to see the other in stark terms: one side is right wing, conservative, homophobic, sexist; the other side is leftist, "progressive activist," nihilistic, anarchical, totalitarian. Issues of freedom of expression, faculty hiring, tenure standards, admissions, course content, and so on, are indicative of rifts in the culture of the university.

Because this little book has been written at Duke University, I think it appropriate to mention that one of the country's first academic freedom cases arose in 1903 at Trinity College, Duke's predecessor. History professor John Spencer Bassett called Booker T. Washington the greatest man in recent Southern history next to Robert E. Lee. Demands were made that Bassett be dismissed. The trustees of the college, however, voted 18–7 in Bassett's favor. Speaking to a large crowd near the campus, President Theodore Roosevelt said: "You stand for Academic Freedom, for the right of [a scholar] . . . to tell the truth as he sees it, . . . and to give others the largest liberty in seeking after the truth." The future of academic freedom depends on how the rifts in the culture of the university are resolved.

I offer my thanks, first of all, to Professor Steven Cahn, the editor of the series in which this book appears, for his patience. He has been waiting for this book for too long a time. I express my appreciation to my colleague Professor William Van Alstyne for the many discussions we have had. I also thank James O'Doherty, my research assistant at an early stage, and Ann McCloskey, my secretary. Finally, to my wife, Naomi—as always—for her intellectual and loving companionship.

Chapter One

Campus Speech Issues

From time to time, the Congress of the United States has considered an amendment to the Constitution that would allow Congress and the states to prohibit the physical desecration of the American flag. Were the amendment to be approved (it would need the vote of two-thirds of each House and three-fourths of the states), it would have the effect of reversing the decision of the Supreme Court in the case of *Texas v. Johnson* (491 U.S. 397 (1989)), which held that a statute designed to protect the flag violated the free speech provision of the First Amendment: "Congress shall make no law . . . abridging the freedom of speech or of the press. . . ." Gregory Johnson had burned a flag in protest at the 1984 Republican National Convention. Yet as Justice William J. Brennan wrote:

> If there is a bedrock principle underlying the First Amendment, it is that the Government may not prohibit the expression of an idea simply because society finds the idea itself offensive or disagreeable.

The Court's decision was met with a great deal of outrage, for as the Court itself recognized, the flag is the "unique" symbol of national unity. Hence the move by Congress to reverse the decision.

This so far unsuccessful move has been met by opposition, much of it coming from people who revere the flag and deplore its desecration. They see the proposal as contrary to the "bedrock principle," perhaps just the thin edge of the wedge toward eroding an essential American freedom. It is somewhat ironic, though, that a number of these same people have no hesitation in supporting campus speech codes. While there may be a difference between a government's restriction of the expression of an idea and a college's or university's imposition of a speech code (a difference that evaporates in the case of a public institution), there clearly is some dissonance here. A double standard seems to be at work. But there are complications. Many people may be more resentful of the government's attempts to restrict free speech than a university's.

1

A university is more of a special-purpose institution, and restrictions on expression, it is sometimes argued, fit in with its aims: restrictions on speech are necessary to promote a "comfortable learning environment." The airing of certain ideas is therefore acceptable, while airing others that are offensive to one or another group is not. Some proponents of speech codes insist that it is not the ideas in the abstract that are of concern so much as "verbal behavior" that may cause hurt. The simplistic old adage, "Sticks and stones may break my bones, but names will never harm me," is rejected. The proscription of certain offensive and disagreeable ideas, or the mode of their expression, is therefore appropriate. Or so it is maintained.

While speech codes have varied in details, these interrelated arguments or sentiments seem to be basic considerations. Another related claim is that punishing "hate speech" teaches people that racism or other prejudice is unacceptable and can bring about tolerance and sensitivity.[1] A school's failure to institute a speech code, it is sometimes said, is tantamount to an endorsement of bigotry and racism. It has also been claimed that the Fourteenth Amendment ("nor shall any State . . . deny to any person within its jurisdiction the equal protection of the laws") mandates that students be protected from demeaning and denigrating speech if they are to be—and feel—equal on campus.[2] At perhaps a lesser level, it has been argued that some Supreme Court opinions legitimize prohibition of certain forms of offensive speech.[3] Whether arguments for speech codes can be sustained is something we examine later.

In line with the above considerations and claims, three basic models of codes have been noted: the fighting words approach, the emotional distress theory, and the nondiscrimination/harassment option.[4] (1) "Fighting words" were forbidden as student misconduct by a University of California code. These are defined as personally abusive epithets inherently likely to provoke a violent reaction whether or not they actually do so, and they constitute harassment when they create a hostile and intimidating educational environment. (2) A University of Texas at Austin code made it a university offense to engage in racial harassment, defined as "extreme or outrageous acts or communications that are intended to harass, intimidate or humiliate a student or students on account of race, color or national origin and that reasonably cause them to suffer severe emotional stress." (3) A third type of code emphasizes "discriminatory harassment." Thus, a proposed code at the University of Massachusetts would have made it a violation for any member of the university community to engage in verbal or physical conduct that the targeted individual or group "would find discriminatorily alters the conditions" for participation in the activities of the university, on the basis of race, color, and national or ethnic origin. The third approach seems the most commonly used, but they all overlap in extent.

Of course, a public college or university, as an agency of government, is required to conform to the provisions of the First Amendment. It is to such an institution that Justice Brennan's bedrock principle applies. In a number of important instances campus speech codes have been struck down by the courts.[5] Private institutions are in a different situation, however. They have more leeway in enacting speech codes.[6] Furthermore, one can easily imagine a church-connected college imposing a speech and conduct code that prohibits on-campus expressions that do not conform to its official beliefs and practices (e.g., opposition to abortion). The courts probably could not disallow such a code, for that may interfere with another First Amendment right, the school's right of "free exercise" of religion.

The similarities and differences that obtain among public, private, and church-connected colleges and universities suggest a broad topic for analysis: the aims of institutions of higher learning. For it is in the context of these aims that arguments for and against campus speech codes take place. Obviously, the topic is too large for full treatment here, but it cannot be avoided entirely. For we are concerned, as it were, with the "constitution" of institutions of higher learning and the extent to which it does contain, or ought to contain, something like Justice Brennan's bedrock principle. In chapter 2, we explore the general rationale of the university's own constitutional free speech provision, namely, the university as a marketplace of ideas.

Also, although the bedrock principle of the First Amendment applies head-on only to public institutions, there is much to be gleaned from some of the debate over how far it reaches. The fact is that not all kinds of speech are constitutionally protected, for instance, obscene speech and terrorist threats. Analogies to free speech jurisprudence are frequently found in the speech code literature, even in the case of nonpublic colleges and universities, many of which proclaim their commitment to principles of freedom of expression and inquiry. That they are found is hardly surprising. While George Washington did not receive the Ten Amendments on Mount Vernon, they nevertheless are as close to being our civil religion as anything. So although the First Amendment applies only to governments and their agencies, we often encounter the complaint of people who have been suspended from a private institution, because of an opinion they have expressed, that their right of free speech has been violated.

The issue of free speech on campus is broader than that of speech codes alone. Speech codes are typically directed at students. Academic freedom, on the other hand, is a concept that applies, first of all, to the corporate, institutional autonomy of a university or college, its freedom to determine who shall teach, who shall be admitted, and what shall be taught. Most importantly, however, it refers to the freedom of the individual faculty member to express his or her views (however unpopular with the trustees or college administration) on extramural matters, e.g., on questions of general or local politics, and freedom from reprisal for positions taken.[7] In this respect, the term refers to free speech "off campus," as it were, though such expression might occur on the campus. The status of tenure is regarded as vital to protect this aspect of academic freedom. In fact, many faculty members do not have tenure, and their protection derives from the respect for academic freedom maintained by the intellectual culture of the university.[8]

In another sense of the term, "academic freedom" is associated with the university as a marketplace of ideas and the free speech provision of the university's constitution, which we discuss in chapter 2. In this sense the term refers to political positions and ideological assertions "on campus," positions and assertions expressed in the course of teaching and class discussion or debate. An instructor in economics might be a proponent of the free market or of Marxism and teach from one or the other perspective, and a student might take a contrary position. With regard to an instructor, the term also covers the freedom (jus docens, the right to teach) of a qualified faculty member to control the contents of his or her courses and research, subject to the limits of professional ethics. Academic freedom in this sense may come into conflict with the institutional autonomy of the university, its freedom to determine what shall be taught. Although trustees and administration should not interfere with academic freedom, that doesn't mean "anything goes." Trustees and administration have the responsibility of seeing that standards of scholarship are not eroded; "academic freedom" shouldn't become a mindless device for avoiding this responsibility.[9]

All these aspects of academic freedom border on the battle being fought over the curriculum and "multicultural education." Although some of the arguments voiced in this encounter are germane to the issue of free speech on campus, they will only be glanced at here.[10] In trying to understand the scope of the university as a marketplace of ideas, we shall, however, consider whether there are grounds for *excluding* a subject or field from the university.

Because of the campus disturbances that were common in the 1960s and '70s, "academic freedom" was extended to include the right of students to attend classes and invited lectures free from disruption by students who disapprove of the ideas being expressed therein. Instances of such disruption have occurred in recent years, as well as in the 1980s. On many campuses, conduct codes forbid disruption of classes and lectures, but these provisions seem to be selectively enforced.

The freedom of qualified faculty members to control the content of their courses can raise a free speech issue in another way, as is illustrated by an item in the *New York Times* (May 11, 1994). Under the headline "A Sexual Harassment Case to Test Academic Freedom," there is a report on events that allegedly took place in a class at the Chicago Theological Seminary. The professor, Gordon Snyder, told a story, from the Babylonian Talmud, regarding a man who falls off a roof and accidentally "penetrates" a woman. The point of the story, presumably, was that in the opinion of the Talmud the man is free from sin because his act was unintentional. (Examination of the source will show that the story has nothing at all to do with sin but rather with whether the man is civilly liable for degradation.) A female student believed that the story justified brutality toward women, and she charged the professor with "creating an intimidating, hostile or offensive environment"—he had engaged "in verbal conduct of a sexual nature." The upshot of the incident was that the professor was severely censured by the seminary and had his course placed under strict supervision.

While it is impossible to comment on this incident without having more information, it is easy to see that the outcome could have a "chilling effect" on the conduct of this course and other courses taught at the school. The ethics of teaching does place limits on professors, and the control that they may have over their courses should not be the same thing as professorial whim. Still, it is plain that sexual harassment regulations can raise campus free speech concerns. And they can raise them for students, too. In fact, there appears to be a trend to use anti-harassment regulations as a way of restricting speech, analogous with prohibitions in Employment Law.[11]

By the beginning of 1995 more than 350 American colleges adopted or tried to adopt a speech code. Although, as noted, the speech-restrictive provisions of codes at several public institutions have been invalidated by the courts, many of them remain on the books unchanged, perhaps for public relations or "feel good" reasons. While some codes appear to be merely aspirational, others designate punishments for violations, anything from censure to expulsion. Offenders (faculty or student) may sometimes also be required to undergo a process of sensitivity training. Sensitivity and diversity training is one of the growth industries on American campuses, bringing with it a corps of (often high-priced) so-called sensitivity and diversity consultants and facilitators. On many campuses such training is a mandatory part of freshman orientation. Some of the practices that have been reported strike me as bizarre; for instance, requiring students to sit quietly while all sorts of slurs are thrown at them. Certain techniques strike me as ethically questionable, to say the least, such as embarrassing or shaming students to the point of tears. If speech codes forbid anything, it should be these sorts of practices.

As objectionable as sensitivity training may be, it raises an important general question: Is moral education part of the university's function, and if so, what shape should it take? More specifically for our purposes, do speech codes have a role to play in the process? The former question raises the large issue of curriculum, which is beyond the scope of this book. The latter question is dealt with indirectly in other chapters. We should keep in mind, of course, that the issue of speech codes is only part of the subject of free speech on campus.

At this point it will be useful to list a number of examples of incidents that are used to raise campus free speech issues. Except for one, all are given here more or less as they are reported in the literature. Almost all of them have occurred in the past ten years. It is sometimes said that the campus speech debate has largely consisted of a rehashing of the same few alleged horror stories whose existence is attested to by anecdotal evidence at best. While a lot of rehashing has occurred, it is my distinct sense that the "alleged horror stories," i.e., incidents of successful or attempted suppression or regulation of speech, are many and not few. But, in an important respect, whether they are many or few really doesn't matter. The incidents raise questions of principle and underlying rationale, which merit discussion in their own right. These questions are the subject matter of this book. Although I shall be looking at real-world incidents, it is not intended as a work of reportage.

(1) A group of students hangs a banner reading "Homophobia Sucks" across the entrance to a building.

(2) A male student wears a sweatshirt with the words "Fuck Women."

(3) One student calls a student who is of Asian descent a "Gook" and says that there are too many of his kind at the university.

(4) In a class on race relations in the United States the lecturer refers to a group as Indians rather than Native Americans. As a result the class is disrupted.

(5) In order to prevent its circulation, a black student takes copies of an independent campus newspaper; a previous issue contained an article about blacks that he found offensive and "full of lies."

(6) A university adopts a rule that prescribes punishment for "derogatory names, inappropriately directed laughter, inconsiderate jokes, and conspicuous exclusion from conversation."

(7) In the campus newspaper, an advertisement is published that denies the occurrence of the Holocaust.

(8) A black student association withdraws its invitation to a speaker who reportedly gave an anti-Semitic speech on another college campus.

(9) A new course proposed by a professor is turned down by the college curriculum committee on the grounds that it is ethnocentric and its syllabus is not sufficiently multicultural. When the instructor objected to such "thought control," her dean declared the objection a threat to academic freedom.

(10) In a legal studies class on the Thirteenth Amendment the instructor refers to the black students as ex-slaves. He is required to make a public apology and attend a "sensitivity and racial awareness" session.

(11) A mathematics professor writes a letter to the student newspaper about date rape; he states that female students who accept invitations to male students' dormitory rooms must bear some responsibility for such alleged rapes. The professor is temporarily suspended.

(12) A professor of biology writes a letter to the student newspaper condoning premarital intercourse between consenting students. The professor is dismissed from his position.

(13) A student newspaper runs a cartoon making fun of affirmative action, for which one of the editors is suspended. A student editor at another school writes an article that criticizes the suspension; he, too, is suspended.

(14) In a project for a course on contemporary issues in feminist art, some women students distribute posters around the university with the names of fifty men chosen at random from the directory, under the heading "Notice: These Men Are Potential Rapists."

(15) A fraternity stages an "Ugly Woman" contest in which one member dresses as a black woman: he wears stringy black hair in curlers, uses pillows to pad his chest and buttocks, and speaks in slang that parodies blacks. As a result, various sanctions are imposed by the university on the fraternity.

Except for one case, the second, these incidents, or incidents like them, are reported to have occurred on North American college or university campuses in the past few years.[12] I used the second case as an example in an undergraduate course. We were discussing John Stuart Mill's defense of free speech in his famous essay *On Liberty*, and I brought up the 1971 Supreme Court case of *Cohen v. California* (403 U.S. 15). Cohen had been convicted in a California court of violating a disturbing-the-peace statute by "offensive conduct." He had worn a jacket bearing the words "Fuck the Draft" in a Los Angeles courthouse corridor. He testified that he did so as a means of informing the public of the depth of his feeling against the Vietnam War and the draft. A majority of the U.S. Supreme Court decided that Cohen's right to freedom of expression had been violated and reversed his conviction.[13]

My class (thirty or so students, mostly seniors, about ten of them women) readily agreed with the result in *Cohen*. Well, I asked, suppose a student wore a sweatshirt emblazoned "Fuck NAFTA" around the Duke campus (the North American Free Trade Agreement was being debated in Congress at the time). Again, my students had no difficulty in saying it should be allowed—a clear case of "political" speech, they said. Well, then, what about a sweatshirt with "Fuck Women"? A brief moment of disquiet could be sensed. Well, what about it? Somewhat to my surprise, given the line being broadcast in many quarters of the campus regarding male-female relations, there was general agreement that this sort of speech or conduct should not be punishable. Even the ten women who were present agreed with that view; at least none of them openly dissented. Unfortunately, I did not pursue the issue. I could at least have inquired whether they thought their view was widely shared by Duke undergraduates. (I think that the general reaction would be quite vocal and negative.) But I was too diffident to press the example. I rarely use the mentioned four-letter word in my own speech, even less in a class, and in more than thirty years of teaching I don't think that I ever uttered it as many times as that day. I did suggest that a generation used to cable television and R-rated movies may have become inured to such language, but that universities and colleges, students and faculty both, perhaps should be held to higher standards of speech and conduct than the rest of society. Because of my diffidence, however, I moved on to other, less discomforting examples. (The concern with single words may seem rather old-fashioned, the sort of thing for which kids would get their mouth washed out with soap. In fact, many speech codes focus on single words, so-called derogatory names.)

Because of my diffidence I also failed to take up a related topic, the possible "chilling" effect on freedom of expression—was my diffidence due in part to that chilling effect? was I committing a verbal sexual assault? will I use this example again in a class? I would not venture to predict whether the students' reaction would be the same, next time.

In order to elicit some of the issues inherent to our subject, it will be useful to look at a few of our opening examples. It will not be necessary to expound each of them with the same degree of detail. Some of them overlap, anyway.

Example (1) is reported as an actual incident at a college in the northeast. A father visiting his son there asked the president of the college whether it would be all right if a group of students hung a banner with the slogan "Homosexuality Sucks" on a college building. "That could never be tolerated," he answered.[14] (As stated, it is not important whether any of this occurred exactly as reported.) Why it couldn't be tolerated isn't clear to me. Perhaps the president merely wanted to avoid dealing with the ruckus that would be aroused. But *shouldn't* it be tolerated? If one banner is the expression of an idea, isn't the other (its opposite) also the expression of an idea? And if it is permissible to express one idea, shouldn't it be permissible to express the other? Various observers of campus goings-on have said that a "double standard" often operates in cases of this kind.[15] Suppose, in example (7) for instance, there is a move to forbid, punish, or (as has been done) severely censure the publication of Holocaust-denying advertisements. Should it matter that they contain blatant falsehoods, as long as they are an expression of ideas? How should such cases be handled?

More fundamentally, though, we need to consider whether there is a principled basis for distinguishing acceptable from unacceptable speech. This is no easy matter, and in the end we may not be able to formulate such a principle, which could be a point of great consequence. Is "Sucks" acceptable on a campus banner, no matter what it is that is supposed to "suck"? The fact is that there may well be levels of unacceptable speech, ranging, as it were, from felonies to misdemeanors. A form of speech may be unacceptable yet not something that should be punishable, as some members of my class seemed to believe in example (2). Is "inappropriately directed laughter," example (6), the sort of thing that should be punished? On one campus a student was suspended after laughing when someone called another student a "faggot" in his presence.

Moreover, much may depend on the context. In the late 1960s and early '70s, expletives and vulgarities were uttered in classrooms in order to cause a disruption; they now are frequently used in student newspapers, and even by some faculty in classes, as a matter of course. But what about "derogatory names"? In example (3), it will be noticed, a derogatory name was directed against a specific person, while in example (10), as described above, the name was used in reference to a group. Should that make a difference to whether a name is acceptable? Of course, regarding these two examples, it could be argued that there isn't much if any difference between them, for in (10), calling the black students "ex-slaves," the name was used in reference to a *present* group. But suppose someone announces more generally that there are too many "Gooks" at the university? Should that be regarded as the expression of an "idea" and hence tolerable, however unacceptable the mode of expression? Suppose the student had merely said that there were too many Asians at the university? The poster with the fifty names, example (14), seems to be the expression of an idea, but does that make it tolerable? If it had said "Notice: All men are potential rapists," would that make it more tolerable?

What makes a name a "derogatory name" anyway? Various kinds of speech (e.g., false accusations) plainly have the capacity to cause harm in a given context. But if, as the old adage has it, "names will never harm me," perhaps what makes a name derogatory and unacceptable is that the recipient of the name finds it *offensive*—it hurts in a way, even if it doesn't harm. Sometimes, however, the recipient may find a name to be offensive while the deliverer does not. Apparently this was the case in example (10); the instructor did not think it offensive to call the black students "ex-slaves," and he did not *intend* to give offense. (In the actual incident, he initially spoke the word to a particular black student who couldn't recite the Thirteenth Amendment to the U.S. Constitution; as an ex-slave, the instructor said, he and all the other blacks should know the amendment's contents. As a Jew, the instructor later explained, he didn't mind being called an ex-slave, for as the annual Passover service states: "We were slaves in Egypt. . . .") If certain words or forms of expression are to be deemed unacceptable and possibly punishable—but only if uttered with an intention to offend—it has seemed crucial to many commentators that there be some standard of offensiveness that is not dependent exclusively on the feelings of those people to whom the remark is directed. For example, some students at a major state university, which had a speech code, complained that they were offended when they were called "rednecks." Some administrators decided that the word itself is not offensive, but were they the right judges?

Examples (10) and (4) should be compared. A number of students in the classroom were upset because the lecturer used the word "Indian" instead of "Native American," and they made it difficult for him to finish out the course. Assuming that there were no Native Americans in the audience who might have taken offense (in fact, I've met Native Americans who prefer to be called Indians), and assuming that no offense was intended, there would seem to have been no wrong committed.

On the other hand, certain words in our language are recognized as intrinsically derogatory names or deprecatory words, e.g., "stupid." Should we say, instead, "cognitively challenged"? These words have negative connotations and express "con" rather than "pro" or neutral attitudes. It is easy to compile a list of them. But the status of many words is far from clear. Perhaps "Indian" falls into the unclear or neutral category, though there are some people who strongly prefer to be called Native Americans, just as there are some people who prefer to be called African Americans rather than blacks. Whether a name has an intrinsically derogatory status will often be controversial, and it might be argued that the recipient, in such a case, just has to tolerate any offense he or she feels. Some words are generally recognized as derogatory and yet do not always cause offense. It is imaginable that someone might not be offended by being called a "nerd." "Zero tolerance" of *any*thing that *any*body finds offensive, which is a principle found in a few campus speech-regulation policies, clearly creates havoc with free speech.

Aside from the problems raised by offensive words and derogatory names, there are perhaps more important free speech issues raised by "ideas" that offend or are unacceptable at least in some sense. For the notion that certain ideas are unacceptable has as its complement the notion that only certain ideas are acceptable. In effect, this duality was noted regarding the banner in example (1), assuming that the expression of an idea was involved. But it is also present in other examples: taking copies of a newspaper (5), the Holocaust-denying advertisement (7), withdrawing an invitation to speak (8), the letters about date rape and premarital sex (11), (12), and the cartoon (13). Though each of these cases probably raises a particular free speech issue, there is in each one an implicit reference to a complementary pair of acceptable and unacceptable ideas.

Consider, for instance, example (13). A student editor was suspended after writing an article criticizing the suspension of a student editor at another school who ran a cartoon making fun of affirmative action. Of course, one can easily imagine that the cartoon was in bad taste, a not infrequent characteristic of the "humor" that pervades college publications. But how significant should that be? It is hard to believe that the second student editor would have been suspended had he written an article *supporting* the suspension. Apparently, advocacy of affirmative action is acceptable but expressing one's opposition to it is not.[16]

This example and the others just cited raise an important and difficult issue about universities. To what extent should they remain neutral as between conflicting ideas and values? Can they in fact be neutral? Isn't the promotion of certain ideas and values implicit in the very concept of a university? Does it matter if a certain idea is regarded as a blatant falsehood? and by whom? Example (7), the Holocaust-denying advertisement, is a case in point. What, in any event, is the distinction between the expression of an idea and the expression of an attitude (the use of derogatory names), and of what relevance is it? Whether there is a workable distinction is, I believe, a crucial question in the campus speech debate. Attitudes generally reflect the beliefs and opinions one holds, which is one reason why outlawing even deliberate attempts at humiliation could be problematic.

Example (15), which occurred at a public university, raises the interesting issue of the speech–conduct distinction. It generally is agreed that conduct (behavior) is more subject to government regulation and restriction than speech is. But it turns out that conduct will sometimes be regarded as a kind of speech and therefore qualify for First Amendment protection—namely, so-called "expressive conduct," conduct that expresses an idea or attitude. Johnson's burning of the flag and Cohen's wearing of the "Fuck the Draft" slogan were held by the Supreme Court to fall into this category. And so did the incident of example (15), according to the federal court that heard the case: "[The] Fraternity's skit, even as low-level entertainment, was inherently expressive and thus entitled to First Amendment protection."[17] Some proponents of speech codes, however, argue in the other direction. They maintain that speech itself can at times be regarded as a form of conduct and therefore become subject to regulation in the way that other conduct is. Should we accept this argument?[18]

We have not discussed all of the examples given in the detail they deserve. The number listed easily could have been multiplied, especially if we include instances of hoax "hate crimes." But enough has been said to indicate the problems, some of which will turn up in our examination of arguments for speech codes in chapters 4 and 5.[19]

What we need to do now is to consider some fundamentals of the "constitution" of institutions of higher learning (colleges and universities, though "university" is the term we shall generally use) and, particularly, why a free speech provision—something like Justice Brennan's bedrock principle—is a vital element of it. Having such a provision, however, does not by itself resolve all the speech issues that might come up, any more than the words of the First Amendment of the U.S. Constitution do. In order to resolve campus speech issues, recourse must be had to the provision's underlying rationale or justification, and even then problems could remain. (It should be kept in mind that speech codes are only one aspect of the topic, free speech on campus.) That rationale is rendered by the notion of the university as a marketplace of ideas.

NOTES

1. See Richard Delgado, "Words That Wound: A Tort Action for Racial Insults, Epithets, and Name-Calling," 17 *Harvard Civil Rights-Civil Liberties Law Rev.* (1982), 148–49. With slight editorial changes and the elimination of some footnotes, this article is reprinted in M. J. Matsuda, C. R. Lawrence III, R. Delgado, and K. W. Crenshaw, *Words That Wound: Critical Race Theory, Assaultive Speech and the First Amendment* (Boulder, Colo.: Westview Press, 1993), 89–110. Three articles from this book are discussed below, in chapters 4 and 5. There is no agreed-on definition of "hate speech," and it is sometimes used interchangeably with "offensive speech." Judging from the literature, though, we can take it to mean: any form of expression (or communication), verbal or nonverbal (e.g., posters, parades, insignia, picket lines) regarded as offensive to racial, ethnic, or religious groups or other discrete minorities (e.g., homosexuals), or to women.

2. See Mari J. Matsuda, "Public Response to Racist Speech: Considering the Victim's Story," 87 *Michigan Law Rev.* (1989), 2320–81. With slight editorial changes and the elimination of some footnotes, this article is reprinted in *Words That Wound*, 17–52.

3. *Chaplinsky v. New Hampshire*, 315 U.S. 568 (1942) ("fighting words," words that "by their very nature inflict injury" and words that "tend to incite an immediate breach of the peace," are not protected by the First Amendment); *Beauharnais v. Illinois*, 343 U.S. 250 (1952) (upholding the constitutionality of a 1917 Illinois group libel law). For a discussion of the erosion of these decisions, see Samuel Walker, *Hate Speech: The History of an American Controversy* (Lincoln: University of Nebraska Press, 1994).

4. See Robert M. O'Neil, *Free Speech in the College Community* (Bloomington: Indiana University Press, 1997), 7–11, for a discussion of the differences. O'Neil's clearly written book covers more topics than we do here, and focuses on public colleges and universities and issues of constitutional law.

5. For an excellent study of the cases, see Timothy C. Shiell, *Campus Hate Speech on Trial* (Lawrence: University of Kansas Press, 1998). The opinion of the court in *Doe v. Univ. of Michigan*, 721 F. Supp. 852 (E.D. Mich. 1989) (speech code effectively declared unconstitutional) is given in appendix A.

6. In February 1995, a judge of the Santa Clara County (California) Superior Court struck down the Stanford University speech code on the basis of California's 1992 Leonard Law: Private educational institutions may not discipline a student "solely on the basis of . . . speech or other communication that when engaged in outside the campus is protected from government restriction by the First Amendment." The Stanford code, enacted in 1990, prohibited "personal vilification of students on the basis of their sex, race, color, handicap, religion, sexual orientation or national and ethnic origin." There is no Leonard Law in other states, but some individual state constitutions contain speech protections that may apply to private colleges and universities.

7. As put in the 1940 American Association of University Professors *Statement of Principles on Academic Freedom and Tenure*: "When they [teachers] speak or write as citizens, they should be free from institutional censorship or discipline. . . ."

8. Academic freedom is a large subject, on which much has been written. See Richard Hofstadter and Walter P. Metzger, *The Development of Academic Freedom in the United States* (New York: Columbia University Press, 1955). A bibliography from 1940 and

articles of historical, legal, and philosophical interest may be found in 53 *Law and Contemporary Problems* (Summer 1990), Freedom and Tenure in the Academy: The Fiftieth Anniversary of the 1940 [American Association of University Professors] Statement of Principles.

9. Academic fields and faculties are generally self-governing and they have the initial responsibility of showing that the "emperor has no clothes." But faculties are notoriously weak (and weak-kneed). The slogan of "academic freedom" too easily becomes a way of avoiding judgments of academic merit. But the issue can have complex dimensions; more about it in a later chapter.

10. I have never met a faculty member who is opposed to the teaching of non-Western cultures, languages, and literatures. What is opposed by many faculty is the ideology and policy of multiculturalism, an expression of which is contained in Stanford University's *Affirmative Action Plan* (October 16, 1991):

> The Office for Multicultural Development is predicated upon the knowledge that our society is composed of independent, multi-racial/multi-ethnic peoples and that our future requires new thinking and new structures which incorporate diversity as a means to harmony, unity, and equity. Moreover, diversity is fundamental to the pursuit of excellence and knowledge. In understanding and accepting this reality, Stanford University begins a transformation to ensure that multiculturalism is infused into (not appended to) all aspects of teaching, research, planning, policies, practices, achievement, and institutional life. It is the mission of the Office for Multicultural Development to develop the multicultural model of the future and guide Stanford University through the transformation.

Cited in David O. Sacks and Peter A. Thiel, *The Diversity Myth* (Oakland, Calif.: The Independent Institute, 1995), 24. The authors demonstrate the dependence of Stanford's multiculturalism on an animus against Western culture and ideals. ("Hey hey, ho ho, Western Culture's got to go!") Statements similar to the one cited are found at other universities.

11. See Shiell, n. 5. This topic is treated in chapter 5.

12. Example (12) goes back to 1960. It is very doubtful that such a letter would result in dismissal today, whether from a public university or from most private institutions. More than likely, it would not be written, and if written, not attract attention. In the 1950s a number of faculty members were dismissed or not renewed because of political positions they had taken, because of failure to sign loyalty oaths, because of political affiliations, or because of refusal to testify before government committees (e.g., the House Un-American Activities Committee) about their political affiliations. I have chosen to focus on more recent examples. Example (12) is mentioned because it reminds us of how much historical context counts, when compared with example (13).

13. At some point in First Amendment jurisprudence, the term "freedom of expression" began to be often substituted for the term "free speech." (Even striptease in bars has been claimed to be constitutionally protected expression.) And once we move to "self-expression," political or nonpolitical, it seems that Mr. Cohen has a pretty good case. As Justice John M. Harlan II said in *Cohen*: "We cannot sanction the view that the Constitution, while solicitous of the cognitive content of individual speech, has little or no regard for that emotive function, which, practically speaking, may often be the more important element of the overall message sought to be communicated."

14. College and university administrations do have a large degree of control over the placement of banners, announcements, posters, etc., on campus property, though that control may be subject to First Amendment free speech guarantees in public institutions. Com-

pare the removal of a Malcolm X mural, with anti-Semitic symbols, from a wall at San Francisco State University. In this instance, the university had paid for the mural, and therefore had the right to remove it. *Herald-Sun*, Durham, N.C., May 29, 1994, G8.

15. Employment of a double standard is a kind of hypocrisy, which occurs when a purportedly general standard is applied in one way to one individual or group and differently (or not at all) to another. Such hypocrisy is not infrequent on college campuses, e.g., when administrations condemn newspaper thefts by some groups but not by others, or when they condemn expression of one controversial idea ("Homosexuality Sucks") but not the expression of another ("Homophobia Sucks").

16. Since a public university is subject to the First Amendment, any allowable restriction (e.g., reasonable time, place, and manner restrictions) on speech must be "view-point neutral."

17. *Iota Xi Chapter of Sigma Chi Fraternity v. George Mason University*, 993 F.2d 386 (4th Cir. 1993). At a nearby university some male students sponsored a contest to find the "Biggest JAP on Campus." "JAP" is a derogatory term referring to a stereotypical Jewish American Princess. I do not know whether the school disciplined these students. JAP baiting incidents have been reported on a number of campuses. Slogans such as ZAP-A-JAP and SLAP-A-JAP have been worn on students' T-shirts, for instance. Compare example (2).

18. See appendix B, Speech and Speech Acts.

19. Example (8) wasn't discussed at all. When the invitation was withdrawn, some people said that the speaker's First Amendment rights had been violated. This claim rests on a misunderstanding. Just as a private association has no duty to provide a speaker with a forum, so may it withdraw an invitation, if there are good grounds for doing so. Regarding example (9), the reader should make his or her own judgment after reading the next two chapters.

Chapter Two

The Constitution of Learning

Public universities and colleges are bound by the free speech provision of the First Amendment, and private universities and colleges, which legally have greater leeway in enacting conduct and speech codes, often proclaim the high value they put on free speech and even their adherence to First Amendment principles. The importance of free speech and academic freedom in institutions of higher learning is, I believe, recognized by many proponents of speech codes as well as by opponents. When speech is restricted, it is well understood that some weighty justification is needed to do so. And we have to begin by asking why free speech is so important.

THE UNIVERSITY AS A MARKETPLACE OF IDEAS

Colleges and universities vary in many ways: some are public, others are private; some are denominational, others are not; some have professional schools, others do not; some have big-time athletic programs, others do not. Furthermore, some emphasize research and others, especially four-year colleges and junior colleges, emphasize teaching. They also differ in their academic offerings: some emphasize the sciences and others feature the humanities with extensive program options. While we should celebrate this variety, these differences do not diminish the importance of campus free speech.

That importance derives from a fundamental idea, namely, that the university is an institution that exists for the dissemination and advancement of knowledge: teaching, learning, scholarship, and inquiry; in a phrase, the pursuit of knowledge by students and faculty. A speech code or other restriction on academic freedom would give notice to applicants and to faculty about the academic environment they can expect to find, just as special programs do. A denominational school that has doctrinal restrictions on academic freedom, for instance, gives such notice.

15

Despite the variety, the university (colleges are included in the term) as a kind of institution is a "special purpose" institution; it serves various social functions, functions that are not served by other institutions or are not served by other institutions in the same way. As a special purpose institution it has an implicit constitution of which a free speech provision is a vital element. (This is largely true of denominational schools too, though as will emerge from the subsequent discussion, they could be losing something of importance if doctrinal restrictions are imposed.) The provision's underlying rationale or justification is rendered by the notion of the university as a marketplace of ideas; however, because of its distinctive characteristics, the university is significantly different from the public marketplace of ideas. This phrase, "marketplace of ideas," derives from an opinion in an important Supreme Court case in 1919.

Jacob Abrams and four other Socialists printed up and threw out from a high window some flyers condemning American intervention in the Bolshevik revolution in Russia. They were convicted under the 1918 Espionage Act of conspiracy to write and publish "disloyal, scurrilous and abusive language about the form of Government of the United States" and to incite and advocate curtailment of arms and ammunition essential to fighting the war against Germany. A majority of the Court upheld the conviction.

Justice Oliver Wendell Holmes, Jr., however, saw the case as one in which these men were convicted for their opinions (opinions that he regarded as silly and repellent). Persecution for expression of opinions, he said, was perfectly logical when practiced by those who had no doubt about their premises. However:

> [W]hen men have realized that time has upset fighting faiths, they may come to believe that . . . the ultimate good desired is better reached by free trade in ideas — that the best test of truth is the power of the thought to get itself accepted in the competition of the market, and that truth is the only ground upon which their wishes safely can be carried out. That at any rate is the theory of our Constitution.[1]

This statement is the source of the popular image of the marketplace of ideas. Although the statement appeared in a dissenting opinion, it came to exercise a powerful influence in subsequent speech cases.

It is pretty well agreed that Holmes's First Amendment rationale is *instrumentalist*; it endorses free speech not as a good in itself but because it promotes discovery of the truth.[2] Its provenance is John Stuart Mill's 1859 essay *On Liberty*. In 1929, in *U.S. v. Schwimmer* (279 U.S. 644), Holmes writes: "If there is any principle of the constitution that more imperatively calls for attachment more than any other, it is the principle of free thought — not free thought for those who agree with us, but freedom for the thought we hate." This is not a tolerance arising out of respect for the other's moral personality. It is rather that the marketplace of ideas does for ideas what the free, competitive market does for material products. It winnows out wrong or silly opinions, just as the market winnows out shoddy widgets. None of this happens all at once in either case, of course, but only in the long run. In the long run, free speech promotes the good that the public should and presumably would ultimately desire, because free trade in ideas promotes discovery of the truth *and* our desires can safely be carried out only when based on the truth.[3] While the context of these decisions is political speech, there is no indication that the rationale is limited to that. Here then is what has been called the Mill-Holmes Thesis: Fight falsehood with truth; fight the worse opinion with the better. Later on I discuss the contention that the marketplace-of-ideas image is a "myth."

The university's constitutional free speech has a similar instrumentalist rationale—free trade in ideas promotes the dissemination and advancement of knowledge—but there is a notable difference between the general public's right of free speech and the university context, to which we shall come.

The university's free speech rationale is analogous to the notion, associated with James Madison, that the "core value" of the First Amendment is not free speech for its own sake but the exchange of ideas on some question of public importance. As Professor J. Peter Byrne has put it: "The conventions of scholarship exist to promote communal discussion of valuable questions, the presentation of evidence and argument in a form that invites response, clarification and correction. . . . [T]his sharing of relevant evidence and the range of arguments we accept as learning."[4]

Byrne's statement is an excellent way of phrasing the "free trade in ideas" in the university context. Communal discussion, which is the matrix of learning and inquiry, presupposes the freedom of speech. And, we should immediately note, many valuable questions, evidence, and argument could deal with matters and opinions that might be regarded by society or some group or individual as offensive or disagreeable. Not only that, many opinions might be just plain wrong. The antidote would seem to be the Mill-Holmes Thesis. In any event, the notion of the university as a marketplace of ideas drives us back to the functions and purposes of schools of higher learning.

Universities and colleges do many things and are expected to do many things. Except for the rare instance of institutions like Rockefeller University, the university is a place where most of its students spend their transitional years from minority to adulthood. It is hardly surprising, therefore, that some commentators think that the university has the ethical mission of preparing its students for democratic citizenship and inculcating in them the highest moral virtues. Statements to this effect are often found in college and university charters. Certainly, many church-connected schools, from which many current universities have grown, are thought to have an analogous missionary function.

Universities are also said to have a "credentialing" function. The degrees they award certify students as having achieved status within a discipline and as ready to ply a trade. In the case of graduate and professional schools, the degree is a "union card" that entitles one to entry into a profession, such as law, medicine, engineering, or teaching. Universities are also thought to be the repository of the achievements of the culture, a conservator of the society's treasures, or an intellectual museum. And perhaps somewhat opposed to this last notion is the conception of the university as the critic, even the radical critic of the culture. This conception can raise the issue of the politicization of teaching.[5]

This list is not complete. All of these items do rest on the fundamental idea mentioned earlier, namely, that the university is an institution that exists for the dissemination and advancement of knowledge: teaching, scholarship, learning, and inquiry.[6] Why, for instance, should the credentialing function itself be given any credence? Why should the university be taken seriously as a critic of culture, if not because of this more fundamental aim? The conception of the university as an institution for the dissemination and advancement of knowledge would be article I or the preamble of the university's constitution, were we to put it in written form.

It is an idea as old as Plato that institutions are brought into existence because of a social need, the fulfillment of which is regarded as a value. With respect to the university, it should be fairly clear what that need is: the *organized* pursuit and dissemination of knowledge. When that need exists, when conditions are ripe, and when human beings put their minds to it, universities are likely to develop. One may say the university is a form of *institutionalized rationality*.[7] Should the need for it fade, should conditions no longer be ripe, and should the effort and commitment decline, the university, as described here, would go under. The shell might remain, but its inner substance would be gone.

The "credentialing function," like other activities (e.g., big-time sports) taken on by universities, may distort or even occasionally corrupt the university's fundamental task—learning. But credentialing is only one reason, and not the only reason, why debates over curriculum and degree requirements are so fierce. Such debates are often in pursuit of self-serving private and disciplinary agendas or partisan political agendas (for faculty, students, and administration). Of course, they hardly are presented as such, and are instead wrapped in the terms of high-minded educational ideologies. Clever people have clever things to say. Few academics will be as open as Professor Wagstaff (Groucho Marx) in the movie *Horsefeathers*. "We want to build a university our football team can be proud of," he sardonically says. The curriculum is hardly the only matter that is debated, but it may well be the most important one. It is one's views on curriculum, in fact, that are most revealing of one's conception of the university.

A CONSTITUTIONAL SINE QUA NON: SPECIALIST FACULTY

The university as a marketplace of ideas, which is the basic rationale for its constitutional free speech provision, is connected to the pursuit of knowledge as essential to the university's mission. A free speech provision may in fact be more central to the university, whose aim is the methodic pursuit of knowledge, than it is to the U.S. Constitution. Before we turn to the process of inquiry, the presentation of evidence and argument on valuable questions—which of course is also part of teaching, there is another element of the university's constitution that requires mention. It will prepare us for understanding how the university's marketplace of ideas is different from that of the general public's.

To speak of the university as an institution is to say that it has established forms or conditions of procedure characteristic of group activity.[8] The group is easy to identify: it is composed of faculty and students and, secondarily, administrators. The members of the university perform in various roles, engage in various activities, in accordance with established forms that define these roles and activities. In the university these roles and activities are given their shape by the university's function, goal, or purpose—the pursuit of learning.[9] How these roles are conceived is therefore rather important.

What characterizes the university teaching and research roles, the dissemination and advancement of knowledge, is that individuals who have expertise in the given subject matter perform them. These people are specialists, qualified professionals, much in the same way that physicians are qualified professionals. And just as physicians are held to professional standards and are expected to exercise a professional judgment, so are faculty members in their teaching and research activities.[10] A specialist faculty and professional standards are basic to the difference between the university's marketplace of ideas and that of the general public's: at an important level, entry to the university's marketplace is restricted in a way that the general public's is not.

Entry for students is on a different basis. Admission to colleges and universities, which we do not discuss here, depends on the student's capacity to learn. Of necessity, much of what is taught and much of what is learned is at the elementary levels of a discipline. In fact, much of the knowledge acquired by students, especially advanced undergraduates and graduate students, is self-acquired. Cultivation of the student's capacity to acquire knowledge and to evaluate it critically (which is best promoted by a rigorous curriculum and core requirements in the humanities and the sciences) is an important aspect of teaching and learning, and so is the stimulation and encouragement of creative thinking.[11] This cultivation brings the student into the marketplace of ideas.

Specialties can, of course, become specialisms. Students and faculty can become highly competent but narrow, with no sense of the larger context of their disciplines, specialists without spirit who are unable to bring to their lives the intelligence that they bring to their own postcollege professional activities. The fault may lie in a distorted view of the university's ideal and an absence of a synoptic view of knowledge.[12]

Nevertheless, teaching and research by specialists are established forms or conditions of procedure in the university. It is the satisfaction of this constitutional prerequisite that gives the faculty, collectively and individually, the intellectual authority to determine requirements for degrees or certificates and what the contents of courses shall be. Because faculty appointment is so important to the notion of the university as a marketplace of ideas, a few words have to be said about it here.

The selection of faculty is primarily the responsibility of faculty, particularly specialists in the relevant discipline. The basic principle is that chemists are to judge the professional qualifications of chemists, historians of historians, and so on. There of course is no guarantee that a qualified specialist, let alone the best candidate, as a teacher or researcher, will in the end be appointed. What is necessary is a good faith attempt, with a responsible exercise of due care, by all participants in the process.[13] The standards employed in the process are the standards recognized by specialists in the given subject, together with the general standards of competence recognized in the university.[14] A similar, apparently circular situation obtains in other professions: qualified physicians (or lawyers) are those people recognized as such by other qualified physicians (or lawyers).

It is not uncommon these days to be told that something sinister is going on here. First of all, the system of faculty appointment has a built-in conservatism, in which originality may go unrecognized; originality might appear as unwarranted deviationism.[15] Well, so it might, unfortunately; some losses will occur. More important, though, is the claim that the whole system of professional expertise and specialist knowledge is a power play in which those in control exercise domination over those who want in. Appeals to "standards" are simply ways of excluding the expression of radically new ideas (and even some old ones) in the academic marketplace. The implication is that the university's marketplace of ideas is a "myth" insofar as entry into the market is restricted.

But the circularity may not be a vicious one. Academic subjects do have a history in which advances in knowledge and a growing sophistication in method and technique are presumed to have occurred. It is the mastery of that knowledge, method, and technique, as they stand at a particular time, that characterizes someone as a specialist. This mastery is not incompatible with originality and eccentricity. And it is the lesson of history that knowledge is not static and that advances in knowledge can take place as a result of research. The charge of circularity, however, is not devastating unless one holds that the idea of advances in knowledge through inquiry is a sham.[16] If this were the case, the university wouldn't deserve to exist at all.

Of course, every subject contains many open and debated questions, and scholars in a discipline may disagree over the answers: Why did the dinosaurs become extinct? What were the causes of the First World War? Was the dropping of an atomic bomb on Nagasaki justified? What is the magnitude of the Hubble constant? Why did the Soviet Union collapse, and why wasn't its collapse predicted by the specialists? And so forth. Nevertheless, this fact need not prevent the recognition of someone as a qualified specialist even by those other scholars who disagree with him or her on some particulars. Experts who hold opposite opinions can still recognize the expertise of their opposition. This point is important for understanding how the academic marketplace of ideas operates.[17]

Not only is it quite clear that standards can be abused, it is also quite clear that sex, race, ethnicity, nationality, and religion should never be allowed to enter into the judgment, pro or con, on qualified specialist status, even if it were perfectly legal for a private university to discriminate in any of these terms. While it may be appropriate for a church-connected school to make adherence to a given religion a necessary condition of appointment in the religion department, it is plainly less plausible for appointments in, say, chemistry. In general, the most effective way to promote academic excellence is a complete nondiscriminatory policy.[18]

The difficulty of the appointments process exists in part because of the close connection between competence and quality, academic merit, and because comparative judgments of quality can be controversial. The position taken here has, however, been attacked by a prominent writer as a form of bigotry.[19] The imputation presumably is that all talk of standards of academic quality and of their nondiscriminatory application is simply a mask for an evil prejudice against women, blacks, and certain other minorities.

The writer in question has also made a more interesting claim. Critics of affirmative action, he is quoted as having said, want a definition of "quality" that excludes considerations of race, sex, and so on. "But once you have subtracted from the accidents of class, race, gender, and political circumstance, what is it that you have left?"[20] The answer, one surmises, is nothing.

Now, what is being implied here? There are a few possible ways of understanding these remarks, and I shall mention only one of them. In asking what there is left—and it is interesting to contemplate what has been left *out*, e.g., religion; political affiliation, as distinct from circumstance—it may be being implied that there never are qualitative differences between candidates other than differences in race, sex, and so on. But this is hard to believe. It would mean that, after subtracting these considerations, there is no difference between an expert chemist and an expert in John Milton. You might as well, then, appoint the literary critic to teach chemistry! It would also mean that there are no differences in academic quality between two blacks or two women. But does being a woman make one a competent computer scientist? does being working class? does being a black computer scientist make one a better computer scientist than a Hispanic—any Hispanic, including a female Hispanic—computer scientist? The implication leads to incoherence. There may be good arguments for affirmative action and preferential hiring (as there may be for having religiously affiliated chemists in a church-connected school), but the one just considered—in effect, a rejection of the ideas of academic merit and quality—isn't one of them.

American universities and colleges (very much in the "genteel tradition") went through a long period in which there was discrimination in faculty appointments against otherwise qualified women, blacks, ethnic Irish, Jews, and members of certain other groups. Being a male, white, Anglo-Saxon Protestant often was a condition sine qua non, and because of this smaller pool, universities and colleges ran the risk of degrading their standards. That they ran the risk of course does not mean that qualified specialists were never appointed (any more than affirmative action necessarily entails that no appointees are qualified specialists). The ideal of excellence in the pursuit of knowledge, however, was often compromised.

THE PURSUIT OF KNOWLEDGE

The conception of the university as an institution for the dissemination and advancement of knowledge by qualified professionals has taken us closer to the university as a *distinctive* marketplace of ideas. Dissemination of knowledge encompasses teaching and other forms of publication, and it covers more than received knowledge but also newly acquired knowledge and knowledge in process. For a fuller understanding of how the university's marketplace of ideas operates we now must deal (however briefly) with the question, what is research or scholarship? We are not concerned with apparatus or equipment, which might vary from field to field. We shall also consider the idea that cumulative knowledge does not apply to some fields, for instance, philosophy and literary studies.

Many people's notion of inquiry is had by way of the comic book image of the wild-eyed, gray-bearded, solitary professor posed over fuming test tubes. But this is a highly distorted image. For while the process can be a very lonely activity, research or scholarship for the advancement of knowledge is very much a *communal* affair. It is again worth quoting Professor J. Peter Byrne: "The conventions of scholarship exist to promote communal discussion of valuable questions, the presentation of evidence and argument in a form that invites response, clarification and correction. . . . [T]his sharing of relevant evidence and the range of arguments we accept as learning."

Research is a communal affair in at least two ways. Consider the comic book image just mentioned. Such an individual might make a "discovery," but the claim has to be supported by *argument* or *evidence*. A claim will not be regarded as an advance in knowledge unless it can survive critical examination—in the context of free trade in ideas—by competent inquirers (qualified professionals).[21] This proposition holds as much for the humanities as it does for the sciences. This is not to say that something necessarily is "final" knowledge merely if it is accepted by the community of specialists, for future inquiry might overturn it. Academics therefore must always retain an attitude of guarded skepticism even toward the most well-attested claims, let alone toward the bizarre and silly claims that are often made, particularly in the humanities and social sciences. Advances in knowledge are provisional, in that better, deeper, and more comprehensive knowledge of a subject or detail might yet be produced. I don't mean to suggest that inquiry and the critical examination of evidence are mechanical activities; both require the exercise of imagination.[22]

Research is a communal affair because the process presupposes results already established by other specialists, which again shows the importance of free trade in ideas. This is most evident in the developed fields. But no research or scholarship is done in an intellectual vacuum. This consideration has an important implication for institutional ethics. Especially because the advancement of knowledge is a communal affair, and because results are disseminated as advances in knowledge, a scrupulous honesty is required. "Don't cheat" is a prime rule of academic ethics: no "cooking the books"; no falsification of data; no misrepresentation of evidence and arguments.[23] The honesty required of the scholar-teacher, an honesty that should be inculcated in students, rules out bias in the search for evidence and in the dissemination of results to other researchers and to students. Perhaps the most insidious form of cheating is politicization, whether in scholarship or teaching, when materials are misstated or distorted in behalf of a partisan cause. An issue, discussed later, is that freedom of speech *seems* to permit lying while the institutional morality of the university forbids it.

Now it is evident, as one is constantly being reminded, that all of us have our biases and prejudices, and great effort may be required to overcome them. In the end, we have to depend on the critical community of scholars to expose bias and prejudice, or at least to show that purported claims to knowledge are inadequately supported, if that is the case. It is also plain that research is often driven by personal motives: desire for advancement, jealousy, etc. Again, we have to count on the critical community of scholars to offset any distorting effects that these might have. We should note that humbugs, phonies, and frauds are not unknown in the real world of universities. Unfortunately, the communal examination of evidence and arguments does not always succeed in unmasking these individuals. More important perhaps is the fact that all research is done with a background of interests and presuppositions, which can always be questioned. This fact is inescapable and raises some difficult questions in the epistemology of scholarship, which cannot be dealt with here.

"Communal discussion of valuable questions" is what characterizes the university as a marketplace of ideas and a community of learning. Teaching and research or scholarship, whether in the sciences or the humanities, has been described as a *conversation*, a conversation between scholar and scholar, teacher and student, and student and student. And it is a conversation to which the presentation of evidence and arguments and their critical evaluation are central, both with respect to the dissemination of knowledge and its advancement. This conversation is the university's marketplace of ideas, and "free trade in ideas" is essential to it. I use the term "conversation" with reservation, though because it suggests laid-back banter, and I have in mind point-to-point discussion.

The marketplace of ideas, as the underlying rationale of the university's constitutional free speech provision, therefore has significance for students as much as for faculty. The mission of colleges and universities dedicated to the pursuit of knowledge is to teach students the modes and methods of inquiry, the major alternative views in each field, and ways to articulate and assess arguments on each side. They will be drawn into the conversation if the university does its job in teaching them how to confront difficult and controversial ideas. They will learn how to engage and challenge their teachers in the critical conversation—though they are often hesitant to do so—as well as other students, in the classroom, in their campus publications and organizations and out-of-classroom discussions. In the clash of ideas and views, the ideas will attain liveliness and interest for the student, and his or her own views will have, as John Stuart Mill points out, a vitality that might otherwise not be present.

Now, it has been questioned whether the idea of cumulative knowledge, and so of advances in knowledge, applies to the humanities. In some fields disputes go on interminably. Philosophy may be the outstanding example—hardly anything ever appears to get settled. There was once a dean at Duke University who would ask candidates for positions in philosophy whether there had been any advances in the field: aren't philosophers still discussing the very same things as the ancient Greeks? But the reason is plain: philosophy's problems are perennially present and they need to be rethought by every age in the light of new knowledge and concerns.

As in the sciences, the humanities are also *about* something. They aim at giving an adequate description, explanation, or analysis of some subject matter, objects, or phenomena. Thus, literary and music criticism aim at giving adequate accounts of certain aesthetic objects (even artistically bad ones), for instance, novels, poems, and symphonies. The phenomena studied in the humanities frequently are complex (think of a Shakespeare play) and are always open to fresh examination from a variety of perspectives.[24] (The same is true of subjects treated in the social sciences.) Yet, some descriptions and analyses can be better than others, as determined by the evidence and arguments offered for them. Of course, some analyses are loony: a teacher of drama at a large university was told to reinterpret some Shakespeare plays "in a new light, so as not to offend feminists." And if it be said that it is "understanding" rather than description or analysis at which the humanities aim, it is still the case that some understandings are better or more adequate than others. With regard to the humanities, the advances in knowledge are these better descriptions, analyses, or understandings, however rarely "finality" might seem to be achieved. And because the results of humanistic research are disseminated as knowledge, seen in these ways, a scrupulous honesty is as required here as in the sciences.[25]

What seems to be behind the claim that there is no cumulative knowledge in the humanities—and, sometimes, that the idea of advances in knowledge through inquiry is a sham—is a radical relativistic postulate, one that has fairly wide currency among "postmodern" humanists and social scientists. Thus it is maintained that "discourse is responsible for reality and not a mere reflection of it." On this latter position, which might be seen as a form of epistemological skepticism, alternative descriptions, analyses, and understandings are never better or worse but are pieces in a political struggle over which ones shall prevail. Scholarship, presumably, is the continuation of politics by other means.[26] The topic is a large one; only a few words can be given to it here.

Now it is of course true that research claims are put forward in language, and if this were all the position amounted to, one could accept it. One could also agree that there are some natural and technical languages that lack the vocabulary for stating certain claims. For instance, the assertions of physics cannot be stated in the language of sociology. Furthermore, one can agree that languages, both natural and technical, are largely inherited and they may well condition what we can say about the world. We do divide up the world largely on the basis of inherited, linguistically formulated categories; language is a "shaper of ideas."[27] But it hardly follows that no way of dividing it up is any better or more fruitful than any other and is just as arbitrary. Suppose a physician were to diagnose someone with a brain tumor. Just imagine telling the doctor that there are other ways of describing the condition. In a trivial sense, that in fact is true, because any event in nature can be classified in an indefinite number of ways. But it does not follow that the physician's diagnosis is inaccurate. If discourse were "responsible for reality," brain tumors could be eliminated by changing our vocabulary.[28]

Despite their differences, the same research standard of advancement in knowledge applies to the humanities as to the sciences: critical examination by competent inquirers of any alleged facts, evidence, arguments, and interpretations put forth.[29]

IS IT A MYTH?

We have been discussing what the marketplace of ideas is in the university and how it ideally operates. Plainly, the university's marketplace differs from that of the general public's, insofar as entry into the former—at the faculty level, though not at the students'—is restricted to qualified professionals who are competent in evaluating arguments and evidence in their field. A professor's classroom free speech right, in fact his or her presence ("access") in the university, is based on *expertise in a discipline.* It will be useful to conclude this chapter by examining the claim that the Holmesian public marketplace of ideas is itself a "myth."[30] We shall want to see how far this claim is applicable to the university.

The basic point of attack questions the very analogy between the economic market and "free trade" in ideas. The efficiency of the market, provision to consumers of the goods they want at the lowest cost, is predicated on the notion of a relatively large number of actual or potential producers and consumers who have access to the market. If a desired item can be produced at a lower cost, someone is standing by who will manufacture it. And if a producer can make a better widget at the current price, consumers will shift their purchases of it to him. All this holds as long as no one, consumer or producer, is prevented from entering or exiting the market. The market is inefficient, however, when anyone holds a monopoly or otherwise dominates the market.

Now what do we find in the so-called marketplace of ideas? Is there open access? In fact, it is argued, this market is dominated by the relatively few individuals and interests that control the media: newspapers, television stations, etc. The marketplace of ideas has a status quo bias, which makes it difficult for "disagreeable" opinions to be voiced, even though they may be true. Put more extremely, the marketplace of ideas, as Herbert Marcuse famously said, is a form of "repressive tolerance," giving the appearance of openness but in fact organized and delimited by those who determine the national and individual interest.[31] Given the way it functions in reality, competition in the marketplace of ideas, from which the truth will emerge, is a myth, especially as regards the fundamental beliefs and practices of society.

Here we have an empirical claim about the workings of the public marketplace of ideas. How accurate is it? Only somewhat, I think. Cranks, crackpots, charlatans, radicals, and hate-mongers seem to have little difficulty (and the Internet has even made it easier; for every nutty idea there is at least one Web site) in getting their ideas before the public—at least to that segment of the public interested enough to find out about them. Therein lies the problem. The marketplace of ideas functions for people *interested* in ideas, just as the market in widgets functions for people interested in having widgets. The remedy proposed by some critics, that newspapers, television stations, etc., be compelled to open themselves up to unorthodox opinions, will not work unless the complacent, uncaring public is also compelled to read or listen to them. But just as I tune out radio stations that play music I don't like, so can I tune out stations that present ideas I don't like. The marketplace of ideas may have an establishment bias that reduces its efficacy in getting unorthodox ideas before the public, but that hardly implies that the image is a total myth.

Now how would the "myth" argument be transferred to the university context? The claim would be, I suppose, that there are academic orthodoxies (reinforced by the system of faculty appointment), established doctrines or dogmas, that inhibit "free trade" in ideas, such that the dissemination and the advancement of knowledge are impeded. This, too, is an empirical claim, and it is a difficult one to investigate. I think there may be some truth to it. For a long time, to give a small example, no English-language scholarly journal would publish articles that disagreed with the picture of Alexander the Great popularized by Sir James Tarn in 1927. The situation now, however, is much changed, no doubt due to strenuous efforts by historians who subjected Tarn's approach to criticism. Apparently, one man's Mede is another man's Persian. What we have in actuality is a good example of how the free trade in ideas works *in the long run.* But, as stated, I believe there is some truth to the claim that there are established positions that impede the operation of the intellectual marketplace. Some people would argue that postmodernism is the current orthodoxy, making it difficult for traditional approaches to be heard.[32]

A second claim about the public marketplace image is that it sees the arena of social discourse as a debating club: it assumes that the participants are rational, capable of fairly weighing arguments and counterarguments, with a view to discovering the truth. But is it the case, as postmodernists might ask, that there always is a truth to be discovered? And even if there is, the falsifications, misrepresentations, and sophistries that freedom of speech (with some limitations) allows hardly get us to it. The public marketplace often seems to be a raucous bazaar rather than an orderly process of truth discovery. It is highly optimistic, even naive, to assume (as Holmes and Mill seem to) that the truth will always or even usually win in the end. If the marketplace actually revealed truth, diversity and conflict of ideas should diminish rather than increase. But this has no more happened than Mill's "experiments in living" have led society to better ways of life. Furthermore, much of so-called liberty of expression has nothing to do with communication of ideas, beliefs, or information but rather consists of appeals to base desire and to emotions of fear, guilt, shame, and envy, of which advertising is the classic case.[33] A similar kind of claim is made in defense of speech codes, discussed later. It would appear, again, that the marketplace image is a myth, a myth that may make us feel good about our political system but a myth nonetheless.

As applied to the real world of the university, I accept that these last considerations do have a grain of truth. Universities do have faculty members, even qualified specialists, for whom "ego" is more important than teaching and inquiry. It is also the case that the communal critical examination of ideas does not always succeed in unmasking sophists, fakes, and frauds, but that doesn't mean it should stop trying. For the First Amendment the discovery of truth is not always crucial to given cases. As the Supreme Court said in 1974 in *Gertz v. Robert Welch, Inc.,* (418 U.S. 323, 339): "[Under] the First Amendment there is no such thing as a false idea." (Basically, this means that any governmental limitation on speech must be viewpoint-neutral.[34]) If there is no such thing as a false idea, there is no such thing as a true one, either. But the proposition that there is no such thing as a true idea cannot be countenanced under the university's regime, which is devoted to the dissemination and advancement of knowledge.

In at least two respects the university seems to have an affinity with the values of liberal democracy. (Very briefly put, liberal democracy is majority rule with protection for individual freedoms.) First, liberal democracy, going back to its Enlightenment origins, esteems knowledge: knowledge liberates man and is, or ought to be, the basis of the state's activity.[35] Second, liberal democracy is tolerant of diverse ideas and their free expression. The two points, it has been argued, are intimately connected, for this tolerance is a condition for the advancement of knowledge and for the critical examination of the social knowledge on which the state's programs are to be founded. But perhaps we should not be too sanguine about this proposition. As even a cursory survey of history shows, great accomplishments in science and philosophy, as in literature and the fine arts, have been achieved in authoritarian societies—but accomplishments have also been impeded.

The university's marketplace of ideas does not operate efficiently when incompetents are appointed, people who are unable to critically evaluate evidence and arguments in their fields or who are unable to convey to their students methods of critical evaluation so that they can participate in it. And it could, perhaps with some exaggeration, be regarded as a "myth" to the extent that academic orthodoxies thwart free trade in ideas, but not to the extent that entry is restricted to qualified professionals. This factor, however, raises a difficult issue: are there any intellectual grounds for excluding some ideas or subjects from the academic marketplace? Can adequate reasons be given for keeping out academic claptrap, for instance? Furthermore, might not speech codes, designed to prevent expressions of the sort itemized in the previous chapter, have an adverse affect on the university's marketplace of ideas? Or can they be justified in any case? These issues are taken up in the chapters that follow.

NOTES

1. *Abrams v. United States*, 250 U.S. 616, 630 (1919).

2. Some commentators hold a *constitutive* justification of the First Amendment. Freedom of speech and freedom of the press, it is argued, are necessary conditions for the legitimacy of government, rather than being merely of instrumental value in promoting honest government or better political decision making or any other good. Freedom of speech is seen as a feature of the citizen's *moral personality*. See T. Scanlon, "A Theory of Freedom of Expression," 1 *Philosophy and Public Affairs*, 214 (1972). Professor Ronald Dworkin, who holds a constitutive justification of the First Amendment, also maintains that an instrumental ground of academic freedom allows too many intrusions; he would rest it on

ethical individualism, the encouragement and protection of individual conviction. "We Need a New Interpretation of Academic Freedom," in Louis Menand, ed., *The Future of Academic Freedom* (Chicago: University of Chicago Press, 1996), 181–98. Dworkin's point is important. Faculty members are deeply committed to their research and teaching, and they may well regard their activities as expressions of their moral personality, which of course should be respected. But it is not the individual's would-be right of self-expression that is important in this process but rather the institutionalized, collective rationality, as it were, of the university in disseminating and advancing knowledge.

3. To follow up on Holmes's economic analogy, might it not be said that a kind of Gresham's Law operates: bad ideas drive out the good ones? Holmes's thought here is that policies based on false social knowledge are bound to be unsuccessful at best and dangerous at worst. This thought apparently has been questioned. Thus, it has been suggested that were it shown that there are substantial, genetically based differences in intelligence between the races, this alleged truth should be suppressed and social policies should not be based on it.

4. 43 *Journal of Legal Education* (1993), 339.

5. For a criticism of the notion of the university as radical critic of society, see Robert Nisbet, *The Degradation of the Academic Dogma* (New York: Basic Books, 1971), 184ff. On "politicization," see n. 14.

6. The modern American research university is not much more than one hundred years old, with the greatest headway having taken place since the end of World War II. (The first university deliberately established as a research university is Johns Hopkins, which opened in 1876, modeled on some European universities.) Of course, there are colleges in which the basic emphasis is put on teaching rather than research. Still, what these schools teach, often quite admirably, is the results that have been achieved by the research universities, and the teachers are people who were themselves trained in such universities. Most faculty members at a four-year college or university are expected to work with students at any level, including those enrolled in specialized courses, advanced seminars, or independent study. Plainly, though, one doesn't have to have a Ph.D. to be an effective undergraduate teacher or have to attend a research university to get a good education.

7. Rationality is a very large topic, and these days a highly controversial one. Rationality has been attacked in a variety of ways: as a form of "domination," as "hegemonic," as "masculinist." We cannot explore the controversy here. By "rationality" we do mean the critical examination, by those who have competence in the techniques of critical inquiry, of evidence and arguments for empirical and normative claims. This definition is meant to be modest, though it will be regarded by us as incompatible with any epistemological position that does not allow for the growth of knowledge. It is only in the latter respect, and no more, that the definition is a "universal criterion." (Compare Stanley Rosen, *Hermeneutics as Politics* (New York: Oxford University Press, 1987), 16: "The Enlightenment, carried through to its logical conclusion, means the suppression of opposition, or a discourse that is 'homogeneous' in its acceptance of a universal criterion of rationality.") The definition is neither an endorsement nor a rejection of foundationalism and its alleged "discourse of domination." We may accept the "historicizing" of knowledge as long as it is compatible with our definition of "rationality."

8. See R. M. MacIver and Charles H. Page, *Society: An Introductory Analysis* (New York: Holt, Rinehart & Winston, 1962), 15. The definition of "institution" goes back to earlier editions of this book and is used by other writers.

9. From our institutional perspective, the function of administration is secondary to that of faculty and students; its role should be the instrumental one of facilitating the learning

done by the other two constituents. Given that universities are organized corporate bodies, holders of property, etc., the administration has many indispensable functions to perform, but it must not lose sight of its primary role. Administrations sometimes pursue agendas of their own (see n. 18) and at other times blow with the wind, readily giving in to pressures that come from other quarters, e.g., vocal student groups. It should be noted that faculty also do a great deal of administration through their participation in numerous committees. Still, despite such service, they often do not have much executive authority over vital issues.

10. Compare the complaint of physicians that as a result of second-guessing by nonprofessionals in health maintenance organizations (HMOs) and insurance companies they are often unable to practice medicine in accordance with professional standards. For a qualified critique of the professionalization of the American academy, see Louis Menand, "The Limits of Academic Freedom," in Louis Menand, ed., *The Future of Academic Freedom*, 3–20.

11. "Although there is no procedure one can teach to guarantee creative thinking, a professor can stimulate creative thinking by challenging students to think about problems they have not thought about before, by showing the students instances of creative thinking which the students may be inspired to emulate, and by providing an environment in which creative thinking is valued and nurtured. . . . If wisdom as creative thinking is taken to be a worthy goal in the academy, professors of the humanities and the sciences share more with professors of the fine arts than is perhaps commonly supposed." Joshua L. Golding, "The Question of Wisdom in the Contemporary Academy," in K. Lehrer et al., eds., *Knowledge, Teaching and Wisdom* (Boston: Kluwer Academic, 1996), 277.

12. The continuing decline of the humanities is both cause and symptom of the distortion, in my opinion. And while I strongly support the study of other cultures (I do not know any academic who does not), so-called multicultural courses trivialize the curriculum when they reduce everything to issues of race, gender, and class. So-called "popular culture" courses, the study of sitcoms, for instance, also run the danger of trivializing the curriculum. Much depends on whether the core of liberal learning remains solid. It may not be too long before universities are valued only for the technical education they provide.

13. See Judith Jarvis Thomson, "Ideology and Faculty Selection," 53 *Law and Contemporary Problems* (1990), 155–76. We should note that it is necessary to distinguish the question of qualifications for appointment to academic posts from the issue of what field an appointment should be *in*. (On the distinction, see Thomson.) Should an appointment be made in computer science or ancient philosophy, given the limited funds available? Should a department of Asian Studies be established? These sorts of questions, which bear on the educational mission of a university or college, are often quite difficult to answer. Compare John Henry Newman, *The Idea of a University* (Notre Dame, Ind.: University of Notre Dame Press, 1982), 74: "[W]hereas it is the very profession of a University to teach all sciences, on this account it cannot exclude Theology without being untrue to its profession."

14. Recall example (7) in chapter 1, the Holocaust-denying advertisement placed in a student newspaper. Such ads are driven by anti-Semitism. Should a candidate for an academic post in history hold such a "revisionist" position, he or she could be rejected, not on grounds of deplorable attitude, but because of incompetence as a historian. See, further, chapter 5. The publication of the advertisement in the Duke student newspaper showed campus free speech ("more speech") at work. The advertisement was countered by one issued by members of the history department which exposed the falsehoods and shoddy scholarship. The Holocaust was vividly brought to the attention of the student body, who

are surprisingly hazy on the subject. (See John Stuart Mill's "vitality" argument for free expression.) Holocaust denial is a prime instance of "politicization," defined by the late Sidney Hook as "the practice of misstating or distorting or denying a truth or judgment for which adequate grounds can be given, in behalf of a partisan political cause, whether it be a revolutionary or a counterrevolutionary one." ("Intellectual Rot," *Measure* (UCRA), February 1989, 1.) Note that Hook, who was himself very much a partisan of political causes, is not rejecting the legitimacy of partisanship. It is sometimes said that the idea that intellectuals should keep their political positions separate from their scholastic pursuits is itself a political statement. Well, perhaps it is, but it's quite a benign one by comparison.

15. Professor Thomson notes the case of Barbara McClintock, whose pioneering work in genetics was not recognized for many years. In 1983 McClintock received a Nobel Prize for discovering "jumping genes" in corn, on which she had published thirty-two years earlier. As to conservatism, the term is not used here in its current political sense. Many departments in the humanities and social sciences are dominated by the radicals of the 1960s and '70s who make entry difficult for political conservatives or more traditional scholars. The tenure system, which cannot be discussed here, not only protects the free speech of faculty members, but also can have the effect of making junior faculty toe the line.

16. There seem to be academics who hold this view. They see the replacement of old ideas and theories by new ones as less than an indication of advance in knowledge and more a function of the fact that holders of the old die off and are replaced by holders of the new. This position often (misleadingly?) relies on Thomas S. Kuhn, *The Structure of Scientific Revolutions* (Chicago: University of Chicago Press, 2d ed., 1970). The idea of advances in knowledge through research does not preclude the occurrence of humbug or cheating. Nor should we assume the whiggish notion that the later ideas and theories are always better than the older.

17. There also are academic subjects in which the disagreements are not merely numerous but also radical. Here, there is more than disagreement on points of detail; there is disagreement on fundamentals, disagreement on proper methods, and even on how the field itself should be construed. Such radical disagreement probably is more characteristic of the humanities and social sciences than the so-called hard, natural sciences. Some fields (philosophy and literary studies are examples) seem to be "inherently controversial" in this way. One side might then consider its opponent as purveying "nonsense on stilts," and dangerous nonsense at that. There then might be an attempt made to keep some field or approach out of the university. In the next chapter, we shall consider how such an argument might go, using the example of sociobiology.

18. Affirmative action programs, which are legion and which exist in many varieties, can put pressure on the appointments process, and pose the danger of compromising standards and excellence—in the case of draconian schemes almost certainly so. Consider the Agenda for Women, as announced in April 1994 by the president of a major public university. After pointing out that women comprise 48 percent of undergraduate enrollments and 40 percent of graduate enrollments at the school, the Agenda states that the number of women faculty has not increased to satisfactory levels, despite increasing pools of women candidates. Among the enumerated goals, presumably to be reached by the year 2000, is that of achieving "full representation, participation, and success of women faculty in the academic life and leadership of the University." "The Michigan Agenda for Women: Leadership for a New Century," Office of the President, The University of Michigan, April 15, 1994, p. 3. If this design were seriously to be implemented, in fields in which there is a shortage of female specialists (and there are many such fields at present, despite increasing pools of women candidates), the only way the goal could be met is by appointing less

qualified candidates. Moreover, unless the size of the faculty were to be drastically enlarged, which is an almost inconceivable prospect, about 1,000 current male faculty members would have to be replaced. In any case, the goal could not be attained unless no more male faculty were appointed for the foreseeable future. Why adopt such an agenda? It has the quality of a "feel good" measure; something is being done, though it is known in advance that it is bound to fail and is certain to cause consternation.

19. The term "bigotry" and its cousin "racism" refer to a complex of strong negative attitudes and false beliefs that are the causes or the effects of the attitudes. By a process of persuasive definition the negative connotations of the terms are often cast on someone who finds faults in a program presumed to benefit a particular racial or ethnic group. Such alleged racism should be distinguished from the real thing, a belief in the inherent intellectual, cultural, or moral inferiority of the group. See Byron M. Roth, "Symbolic Racism: The Making of a Scholarly Myth," *Academic Questions* (Summer 1989), 53–65.

20. Quoted in Dinesh D'Souza, *Illiberal Education* (New York: Free Press, 1991), 176. The writer in question is my former colleague, Stanley Fish.

21. This statement is not put forward as a definition of "knowledge." Rather, it is an assertion about when a claim is considered to be an advance in knowledge in the university context. Moreover, to say that advancement of knowledge is a communal affair is *not* to say that knowledge is a "social construction."

22. This paragraph, admittedly, elides a number of pivotal issues. First of all, it cannot be assumed that *all* competent investigators will always agree over results, especially in the humanities and social sciences but even in the natural sciences. One could (in Peircean fashion) define "truth" as what the community of competent inquirers will *ultimately* agree on. I have deliberately avoided using that term. I am concerned with the advancement of knowledge, reaching a level that is better, deeper, and more comprehensive than what preceded it. Admittedly, though, the concept of truth is required to explicate this notion. Second, I do not assume that the scientific method is the only legitimate mode of critical examination. (If I understand him correctly, on this point and some related points I depart from the excellent book by Jonathan Rauch, *Kindly Inquisitors* (Chicago: University of Chicago Press, 1983).) Crucial to the above account, of course, is the idea that advances in knowledge are possible.

23. These points concern the "internal morality" of research or scholarship; the "external morality" of research, the extent to which its impact on society for good or ill should be a factor in determining research programs, is not under consideration here. It should be noted that research paid for by agencies external to the university, e.g., business and government, is potentially corrupting of the university's ideal. It was assumed at one time, perhaps unrealistically, that the results of inquiry should be freely shared, and that they would be distributed to all interested parties through publication in specialist journals. The fact that some discoveries are patentable, can be "owned," has changed the situation. Patent and copyright spur inquiry but also restrict the marketplace of ideas.

24. Of course there can be controversy over approaches and methods of analysis, but positions have to be argued. See, for instance, Stanley Fish's vigorously argued critique of the New Criticism in his book *Is There a Text in This Class? The Authority of Interpretive Communities* (Cambridge: Harvard University Press, 1980).

25. There is, however, a side to the humanities to which many people are loath to attribute the name of knowledge. This is their evaluative or normative side. Literary criticism, for instance, aims not only at an adequate description or analysis but also at an evaluative judgment, a judgment of artistic worth. Such judgments, it is said, do not deserve to be called knowledge; they ultimately are matters of taste. Nevertheless, evidence and argu-

ments are presented for them, which can be critically examined by those who have competence in the techniques of critical inquiry. The same holds for judgments in moral philosophy, normative economics, and the so-called policy sciences.

26. For a more extensive discussion, see Jerry L. Martin, "The University as Agent of Social Transformation: The Postmodern Argument Considered," in Howard Dickman, ed., *The Imperiled Academy* (New Brunswick, N.J.: Transaction Publishers, 1993), 203–37.

27. Benjamin Whorf, *Language, Thought, and Reality*, J. B. Carroll, ed. (Cambridge, Mass.: MIT Press, 1988), 212.

28. The globally skeptical doctrine, too briefly discussed here, should be compared with locally skeptical "labeling theory," which is found in certain fields. Thus, in the area of psychiatry it has been maintained that "mental disease" or "mental illness" is simply what we have chosen to label as such, there being no objective condition designated by the term. See Thomas S. Szasz, *The Myth of Mental Illness* (New York: Harper & Row, 1963), *The Manufacture of Madness* (New York: Harper & Row, 1970), and other works; Michel Foucault, *Madness and Civilization* (New York: Pantheon Books, 1965). This kind of thesis must be established empirically in particular, defined kinds of cases; it cannot be argued purely on a priori grounds.

29. I am not claiming that there is an identity of method in the humanities and the sciences but only a fundamental similarity. The "warfare" (*Methodenstreit*) between the natural sciences and the humanities goes back to the nineteenth century and was more recently revived in a somewhat different form by C. P. Snow's Rede lecture, *The Two Cultures and the Scientific Revolution* (Cambridge: Cambridge University Press, 1959).

30. The seminal piece is Stanley Ingber, "The Marketplace of Ideas: A Legitimizing Myth," 1984 *Duke Law Journal*, 1–91.

31. Marcuse maintains that this repressive tolerance is a false tolerance; we should tolerate only the truth. See his essay in *A Critique of Pure Tolerance*, by R. P. Wolff, B. Moore, and Herbert Marcuse (Boston: Beacon Press, 1965). As Sidney Hook argues, this is a denunciation of totalitarianism on the grounds that it is the wrong kind of totalitarianism. Sidney Hook, *Academic Freedom and Academic Anarchy* (New York: Cowles, 1969, 1970), 172ff.

32. See, for instance, various articles in Howard Dickman, ed., *The Imperiled Academy*.

33. Advertising (commercial speech) does have some degree of First Amendment protection. "[The] relationship of speech to the marketplace of products or of services does not make it valueless in the marketplace of ideas." *Bigelow v. Virginia*, 421 U.S. 809 (1975). Restrictions that would not be tolerated with respect to certain other kinds of speech may however apply to commercial speech, as determined by a set of tests, for which see *Central Hudson Gas & Elec. Corp. v. Public Service Comm'n*, 447 U.S. 557 (1980).

34. In other words, an officially sanctioned truth is disallowed. For example, a law forbidding discussion of race would violate content neutrality; a law forbidding advocacy of black supremacy would violate viewpoint neutrality.

35. The idea that knowledge liberates man has early roots, and it was particularly prominent in the Enlightenment, which put the emphasis on scientific knowledge. Scientific knowledge is of course indispensable, but to the extent it is taken to mean that all human problems can be solved by the sciences ("scientism"), I would reject it. It should be noted that Enlightenment ideology has had authoritarian manifestations particularly in some of their left-wing variants, e.g., "official Marxism." The secularism of some Enlightenment thinkers also exhibits antireligious authoritarian forms, from which I would want to disassociate myself.

Chapter Three

Campus Speech and Unacceptable Ideas

We have seen that free speech is indispensable to universities and that its underlying rationale is the notion of the university as a marketplace of ideas, for the promotion of knowledge through learning and inquiry. Any restrictions on speech, whether by way of a speech code or an academic orthodoxy, would have a strong burden to overcome in order to justify them. But perhaps such restrictions can be justified. The marketplace-of-ideas rationale, as noted, is instrumentalist, and the goal of knowledge, as worthy as it is, might have to give way to other worthy goals or values that allow for restrictions.[1] Recall that Justice Holmes saw "free trade in ideas" in terms of truth-discovery. Well, suppose the police want to extract the truth from someone suspected of committing a crime. Would they be justified in torturing him in order to get it? Generally, no: getting the truth is not worth the harm inflicted by torture and the indignity to moral personality. (But suppose the individual refuses to reveal where he planted a bomb. Wouldn't torture then be justified to get him to tell?) University ethics committees do in fact impose limits on the pursuit of knowledge, particularly when research on human subjects is involved.

"DANGEROUS" IDEAS IN THE MARKETPLACE OF IDEAS

These considerations point to a sort of criticism of the Holmesean marketplace-of-ideas notion different from that discussed in the previous chapter—"myth," a normative rather than empirical sort. The marketplace image, it is argued, sets the value of truth higher than other social interests. Taken together with its philosophical underpinnings, the image implies, in the interests of truth discovery, the utmost feasible freedom of expression up to a "clear and present danger" of substantive evils that the government has a right to prevent, as Holmes put it.[2] This position has drawn the following remarks from the late Alexander M. Bickel, a distinguished writer on constitutional law:

> [Holmes] did admit that all ideas carried the seed of future dangers as well as benefits. His answer was this: "If in the long run the beliefs expressed in proletarian dictatorship are destined to be accepted by the dominant forces of the community, the only meaning of free speech [—*the only*—] is that they should be given their chance and have their way." If in the long run the belief, let us say, in genocide is destined to be accepted by the dominant forces of the community, the only meaning of free speech is that it should be given its chance and have its way. Do we believe that? Do we accept that? . . . Where nothing is unspeakable, nothing is undoable.[3]

This is the place, Bickel goes on,

> at which one asks whether the best test of the idea of proletarian dictatorship, or segregation, or genocide is really the marketplace, whether our experience has not taught us that even such ideas can get themselves accepted there, and that a marketplace without rules of civil discourse is no marketplace of ideas, but a bullring.[4]

The brunt of Bickel's remarks is that catastrophically dangerous and evil ideas imaginably could be implemented in a democracy, and it would be wrong and foolhardy to wait to prevent their airing and advocacy only when they begin to be acted on.[5]

Unfortunately, Bickel doesn't state what these rules of civil discourse are. Of course, a bullring is no place to have a civil discourse, especially if the bull and the matador are intent on killing each other. Of course, a discussion between opponents requires adherence to some rules, if the parties hope to convince each other or if they hope to find some mutually acceptable goal. It may be the case that certain conversations rest on a "contract" of civility and politeness.[6] Formal debates, furthermore, have governing "rules of order" which prohibit irrelevancies, and so on, but which, however, do not apply to the public marketplace, where almost anything goes. The citizen's free speech right is not subject to "rules of order" that would prohibit irrelevancies, distortions, and even (with some exclusions) outright falsehoods. But it is far from clear that this is all Bickel has in mind. Rather, he seems to be thinking of ruling out expression of certain potentially dangerous ideas, which would be allowed in an unfettered public marketplace.

Turn now to the university. Let it be granted that the communal, critical examination—in teaching, research, or discussion among students and among professors—is best conducted in an atmosphere of civility and politeness (though it is sometimes regarded as uncivil and impolite to criticize somebody's opinion or thesis). But should the expression of certain ideas be suppressed or censored because some individual or group finds them offensive, dangerous, or just plain false?

On American campuses open advocates of genocide seem to be extremely rare, at least I haven't heard of any, aside, perhaps, from the neo-Nazis who occasionally show up and the preachers of anti-Semitism who come pretty close to it. I think there are some defenders of proletarian dictatorship, though the defense usually takes an indirect form. As to segregation, we don't hear the blatant kind of advocacy that was not uncommon forty or fifty years ago. There in fact are a number of other ideas, beliefs, and opinions (including some scholarly ones) whose absence from the campus would not be greatly deplored by me. But the situation is not so simple.

If we don't approve of open advocacy, does that mean we should also try to suppress discussion of unacceptable ideas, whether in courses or scholarly publications? Consider genocide. There has been a long-standing debate over the meaning of the term and what it exactly covers.[7] Some instances of mass slaughter have not been regarded as genocide by various participants to the debate, and their opponents hold them to be defenders of genocide. Instances of large-scale killings now going on in various places are regarded by some people as genocide and by others as inevitable incidents of civil war. A discussion of genocide could change someone's views on the scope of the term, to the point that his opponents might come to regard him as an advocate of the practice. In any event, suppression of discussion of genocide could be viewed as an exercise in "thought control."

Segregation is even more complicated. When the 1954 Supreme Court decision in the desegregation case *Brown v. Board of Education* (347 U.S. 483) came down, the Court's reasoning was criticized by a number of liberal constitutional scholars, who were in turn attacked as defenders of segregation. The issue of segregation has its near relatives today. Some college campuses have separate dormitories for blacks, Asians, and Hispanics, and critics maintain that this is a reinstitution of segregation. Are they right? Any discussion of the issue is further complicated by the introduction of the terms "racism" and "institutional racism." These days, anyone who finds faults in a program presumed to benefit a particular racial or ethnic group can end up being called a racist. So, critics of affirmative action have been denounced as racists, though they reject the appellation.

Plainly, an open discussion of affirmative action, in classes or academic articles, will have to go into its pros and cons, with the risk that some people might change their minds. In context, there may be a very thin line separating advocacy and discussion. Shall discussion of affirmative action be suppressed or censored because someone might come out on the "wrong" side? Again, the specter of thought control rears its head.

Consider finally church-connected schools. They may want to keep the purity of their beliefs. But unless they rule out all discussion of contrary views, which they usually do not and cannot do, they too have to run the aforementioned risk. In general, then, a marketplace of ideas of some degree will operate whenever some belief or opinion is discussed, no matter how "unacceptable."

Nevertheless, these considerations do not end the topic of restrictions on campus speech. For it might still be the case that as much as discussion of any subject is allowed, a speech code could have a "chilling effect" on it, perhaps to the point of permitting expression only of the "right" position. Second, there is a sort of discussion that might take place which is designed to argue that some subject, course, or research program should *not* be allowed within the precincts of the university, because of the ideas it involves.

As was pointed out in the discussion of the examples in chapter 1, a number of them can be seen to involve the expression of ideas. Even in the absence of a speech code the campus atmosphere might chill their expression. Thus example (1): A banner with "Homophobia Sucks" is acceptable but not one with "Homosexuality Sucks." On many American campuses today there are programs, demonstrations (Blue Jeans Day, at Duke University), and courses (Queer Studies), in which so-called homophobia is roundly criticized and homosexuality vigorously defended, but campuses that promote a contrary view (e.g., Bob Jones University in South Carolina) seem extremely rare. Admittedly the topic is highly emotionally charged, and an open classroom discussion of homosexuality is probably impossible at present, even under rules of civil discourse.

Aside from atmosphere, a speech code clearly could have a chilling effect on discussion. At one state university a student was subjected to a formal disciplinary hearing for violating the policy against speech that "victimizes" people on the basis of "sexual orientation." In a class discussion he had said that he regarded homosexuality as a treatable disease. Apparently, his belief wasn't "right," and under this regime others holding his opinion would be rather cautious. Granted, some speech codes have been constitutionally invalidated for public universities, and it may no longer be possible to subject someone to discipline there for such an offense; but many such codes remain on the books, telling students what sorts of expressions and ideas are "unacceptable." Even where codes are nonexistent, freshman orientation sessions are often used to accomplish that end.[8] And in any case, what about a private institution, which may still have a speech code? We shall come back to speech codes later, to see whether they can be justified despite their chilling effect on free trade in ideas.

EXCLUSION OF IDEAS FROM THE UNIVERSITY?

We have already noted that academic orthodoxies and dogmas may impede the operation of the marketplace of ideas. Though we cannot examine this large and difficult topic here, it is plainly the case that many universities are not hospitable to certain subjects, courses, or research programs because of ideas they involve.[9] In the 1930s and '40s Duke University was a center for psychical research, but it is pretty clear that parapsychology would be a nonstarter there today. Parapsychology is regarded by very many faculty as a pseudo-science, and one can easily think of other subjects that would be put in that category. There also are various subjects, notwithstanding their scholarly trappings, that many academics would regard as being of dubious academic worth, in fact as spurious fields that do not belong in the university. So-called ethno-obstetrics may be an example.

If exclusion from the university is not to be based on a sheer academic orthodoxy, it will have to be based on an argument, an argument that appeals to academic grounds, which obviously are quite different from financial reasons for excluding a subject. Exclusion on academic grounds is not a violation of the university's marketplace of ideas, though it would be of the public's, where anything goes. As an illustration, we shall in the next section briefly look at an attack on the field of sociobiology, and consider some of the issues it entails. The attack was designed to show that sociobiology lacked academic respectability. Somewhat ironically, in an important speech code case it was claimed by a university lecturer that the code affected the contents of his courses in a field allied to sociobiology.

In 1988, the University of Michigan adopted the Policy on Discrimination and Discriminatory Harassment, which prohibited "any behavior, verbal or physical, that stigmatizes or victimizes an individual on the basis of race, ethnicity, religion, sex, sexual orientation, creed, national origin, ancestry, age, marital status, handicap, or Vietnam-era veteran status." This policy was challenged in court by a lecturer in biopsychology on the grounds that it infringed on his freedom to teach, because class discussion of theories of biologically based differences between the races or sexes might be taken to violate the policy. In a detailed opinion the court (*Doe v. University of Michigan*) found the Michigan Policy to be unconstitutional, a violation of the First Amendment, on grounds of vagueness and overbreadth.[10] ("Congress shall make no law . . . abridging the freedom of speech, or of the press. . . .") Similar findings have been made regarding other campus speech codes.

While the lecturer won his case, the court's decision had nothing in particular to do with the contents of his courses. The court did not take up, and quite properly so did not, a rather fundamental question, namely, the academic respectability of biopsychology, whether biopsychology (or any other field, for that matter) belongs in the university in the first place.[11] The question of academic respectability falls to the university for a determination. This much is affirmed in the 1957 concurring opinion of Justice Felix Frankfurter in *Sweezy v. New Hampshire*.[12] Quoting from another source, Frankfurter (a former academic) identified "the four essential freedoms of a university—to determine for itself on *academic grounds* who may teach, what may be taught, how it shall be taught, and who may be admitted to study" (emphasis added). State legislatures and federal law, too, have in fact intruded on all of these "essential freedoms." Frankfurter, however, does not spell out what these "academic grounds" are.

Normally, of course, "what may be taught" and "how it shall be taught" are matters to be decided on by the experts, the qualified professionals in a field. Academic traditions will also be a factor. But suppose the academic status of a subject is controversial? Then the issue has to be decided by a communal critical discussion, in which arguments and evidence are presented.[13]

AN ILLUSTRATION: THE ARGUMENT OVER SOCIOBIOLOGY

Because a discussion of academic respectability would be unsatisfyingly abstract without an illustration, let us briefly turn, then, to sociobiology, the debate over which is in many ways a paradigm of debates over other subjects. Sociobiology is the investigation of animal behavior from the perspective of natural selection.

Sociobiology, it appears, was the object of a concerted effort to discredit its academic credentials.[14] We cannot go into great detail, and we only consider two general sorts of criticisms that were made early on in the controversy, from which some useful general suggestions may be derived on what "academic grounds" are. The dispute conveniently may be dated to the publication of Edward O. Wilson's book, *Sociobiology: A New Synthesis*, in 1975, of which the last chapter is devoted to speculation about sociobiology's application to humans.[15] In some respects the dispute revives the old nature/nurture debate.

The two sorts of criticisms are *conceptual–methodological* and *moral–ideological*. The first sort is basically "scientific," and we shall list the criticisms without much discussion, though if valid they are very powerful. The second sort is closer to matters discussed above. In fact, much of the attack on sociobiology derives its motivation and vehemence from it.[16]

What are the respective contributions to human conduct of nature and nurture, or, in current terms, of genetics and the environment? In the case of nonhuman animals it seems plausible to say that their behavior and social organization are determined by their genes. (Thus, an explanation in terms of genetic selection may be given of the fact—if it is a fact—that male birds, unlike mammals, frequently get involved in child care.) And it is not uncommon for sociobiologists to draw an analogy between human beings and ants. (E. O. Wilson, the leading figure in sociobiology, is considered the world's expert on the behavior of ants.) As one proponent of sociobiology has said, "If the social behavior of ants can be understood at the level of genes, so can the social behavior of people." Such statements have been taken to suggest that various human practices and institutions are as genetically determined as the behavior of ants and can be changed, if at all, only by paying a heavy "cost." If true, sociobiology would have significant implications for social policy.

Conceptual–methodological flaws

To counter the sociobiologists' approach, the critics directly attack their adaptationism and genetic determinism. A major claimed difficulty concerns the descriptions of behavior employed by sociobiologists. When the sociobiologist characterizes some behavior, of an animal or a human, as defending its territory, as rape, as xenophobia, as incest-avoidance, as altruism, as self-sacrifice, how good is such a description? And if an explanation can be given in terms of natural selection for an animal, can it be extrapolated to human behavior? Sociobiology, it is claimed, is seriously flawed, conceptually and methodologically, on these matters.[17]

The sociobiologist has his responses. Let us just consider the issue of altruism. In Wilson's book *Sociobiology: A New Synthesis*, he designated altruism as the central theoretical problem of sociobiology: "How can altruism, which by definition reduces personal fitness, possibly evolve by natural selection?"[18] Behind this question is the rejection (by biologists generally, though not by Wilson entirely) of group selection, the idea that evolution is shaped by competition among groups of animals as well as among individuals. Instead, it is held that only individual genes reproduce themselves in a manner for natural selection to work; selection works to preserve characteristics helpful only to the individual. Genes, as one sociobiologist says, are "replicator" units with the sole purpose of replicating and getting into the next generation. The organism as a whole functions in the manner of Samuel Butler's chicken: the chicken is the egg's way of making more eggs.

But if this is the case, how can we explain how self-sacrifice aids in the process of natural selection? The individual animal that subjects itself to extinction by giving a warning call is not going to get more of its genes reproduced in more off-spring. How then, it is asked, can altruism, which by definition reduces personal fitness, possibly evolve by natural selection? And, we might ask, does "altruism" designate a single form of behavior whose presence requires an evolutionary explanation?

To deal with this question and other related questions, the sociobiologists intro-duce the concepts of kin-selection (or inclusive fitness), reciprocal altruism, and indirect reciprocity. For instance, the animal that gives the warning call has kin to which it is genetically related, and it leaves more offspring, so to speak, by help-ing its kin survive to reproduce. The adverse effect on personal fitness is offset by its effect on kin. Reciprocal altruism explains why we do things for strangers: I do things for you in the expectation that you will do things for me. And indirect reciprocity explains altruistic behavior toward members of one's society even when they are unrelated to one and when there is small chance of being benefited in return; if you don't benefit me you might still benefit my kin.

Are these concepts adequate to handling the problem? I don't know, and I am not interested in criticizing or defending sociobiology. Our point lies in another direction.

Plainly, we don't want falsehoods taught in the university. Quite often, though, we don't know whether a given hypothesis or normative judgment is true or war-ranted. Inquiry is then necessary in order to establish its status. But, very likely, every field contains *some* falsehoods. Being riddled with falsehoods is entirely another matter, and this is shown, if at all, by demonstrating fundamental con-ceptual–methodological flaws in an approach. The sociobiologist, of course has his responses (as in the case of altruism), so the debate continues in the univer-sity's marketplace of ideas, in the broad community of competent inquirers.

The upshot of the attack on sociobiology is that the field is riddled with false-hoods. As noted above, the criticisms, *if valid*, are very powerful. And nothing can be more devastating to the academic respectability of a field than its being riddled with falsehoods. This point is what the example of sociobiology is meant to illustrate: it suggests one way of how we are to understand opposition to a sub-ject on academic grounds.

Moral–ideological flaws

The second sort of argument takes us back to matters mentioned earlier. The claim now is that sociobiology supports "unacceptable" beliefs, attitudes, and practices, such as capitalism, racism, and sexism, which explains the vehemence of the attack.

Briefly put, the nub of the charge of moral–ideological flaw is that hypotheses that attempt to establish a biological basis of social behavior "tend to provide a genetic justification of the status quo and of existing privileges for certain groups according to class, race, or sex."[19] (Recall, here, the *Doe* case.) As did German "racial science," sociobiology provides a moral justification of racism, viewing a group as morally inferior. The complicity of German academics in Nazi projects was established as early as 1946 by Max Weinreich in his undeservedly neglected book, *Hitler's Professors: The Part of Scholarship in Germany's Crimes against the Jewish People*.[20] (Rudolph Hess, a leading Nazi, said in 1934 that National Socialism was simply "applied biology.")

Two critics of sociobiology summed up the claimed moral–ideological flaw as follows:

> During the 1970s genetic determinism led to the formation of a new discipline called "sociobiology," demarcated in particular by the publication of E. O. Wilson's book, *Sociobiology: A New Synthesis*, in 1975. The existence of genes for aggression, territoriality, and intelligence was claimed. As these behaviors are all characteristic of the stereotypical male in Western capitalist society, sociobiology reinforces the "naturalness" of patriarchy. It also "explains," and so condones, the existence of violence in society. The latter, coupled with belief in genetically determined race differences in IQ, allows sociobiology to sanction racism as well as sexism. It provides apparent scientific rationale for the existing social order. Put another way, it offers a genetic, and therefore fixed explanation for social difference and justifies the continued domination of one group by the other. . . . The terminology of capitalism is commonly used, and the ideology of individualism is clearly apparent. It offers capitalism feedback in the form of biological justification.[21]

Here, then, is a second suggestion as to how we might understand opposition to a subject on academic grounds. However, this sort of argument is subject to two possible interpretations. The first possibility is somewhat along the lines of the former type: sociobiology supports a set of false or unacceptable moral–ideological conclusions and, hence, must itself have false theses, itself be a pseudo-science. What we have is a kind of *reductio ad absurdum* argument against sociobiology: *because* it supports false or unacceptable moral or political opinions, it, too, must be false. One could then maintain, on academic grounds like those discussed above, that sociobiology has no place in the university.

Now, for all I know there may well be sociobiologists who believe that their field does support capitalism, patriarchy, sexism, and, as did German "racial scientists," the moral inferiority of some races. But would they be right? Do various sociobiological hypotheses provide a moral justification of racism, say? If these hypotheses were true, would they justify racism? And *assuming* for the sake of discussion that sociobiology does, in some way, lend support for the view that some races are "morally inferior" to others, does that show that sociobiological hypotheses are false? Is it the case, as a general matter, that a field that has the moral–inequality consequence, as detractors of sociobiology claim of it, must be false and cognitively shoddy?

The last question raises general philosophical issues that cannot be taken up here. What, for instance, does it mean to say that one race is "morally inferior" to another, and how could empirical claims "lend support" to such a view? For instance, suppose it could be demonstrated that average IQ differs between races. Would that fact show that one race is "morally inferior" to another? Is a person with an IQ of 100 morally inferior to someone with an IQ of 150? It seems to me, rather, that the notion of the moral inferiority of a race can, and should be, controverted on moral grounds.

But it also seems to me that the purported fact that some field of inquiry might lend support to racists does not *of itself* show that the field is riddled with falsehoods. Political, moral, and ideological criteria do not determine scholarly (or artistic) merit and truth anymore than the fact that T. S. Eliot was an anti-Semite shows his poetry is bad or that Joseph Conrad arguably was pro-colonialist shows he is a bad novelist. (This does not mean that moral criticism of the arts is necessarily mistaken.) The quality of the writing, good or bad, has to be established independently. Analogously, so does the falsity of sociobiological hypotheses.

By contrast, a second way of understanding the moral–ideological argument does not necessarily involve the assertion that sociobiology is riddled with falsehoods. Rather, it is a direct condemnation of sociobiological hypotheses because, if true, they *do* provide empirical support for capitalism, patriarchy, and the moral inferiority of some races. (If the crucial hypotheses are false, as is perhaps shown by the conceptual–methodological argument, they do not provide such support. What is crucial perhaps is that they are *believed*, by proponents or opponents, to provide such support.) Sociobiology, therefore, is not academically respectable because it supports (or is taken to provide support for) "unacceptable" moral–ideological ideas.

On this way of understanding the moral–ideological argument, sociobiological hypotheses, if true, in effect are "dangerous truths" (but see below) because of the morally or politically unacceptable propositions they presumably support. But shouldn't purported dangerous truths and subjects be discussed in courses and scholarly gatherings and be researched in the university? If not there, where else? Many academic disciplines (e.g., economics, psychology, history, and even philosophy) seem to contain dangerous truths, though not necessarily ones about alleged "moral inferiority." And who knows what other subjects might turn out to contain yet unforeseen dangerous truths?

It is rather clear that the authors of the above long quotation have a strong animus against capitalism, but it is less clear what they do support. Is it perhaps proletarian democracy? But we saw earlier that Alexander Bickel apparently thought that proletarian democracy was a dangerous doctrine that should be suppressed or censored. In any event, the university is precisely the place where the virtues or vices of capitalism, proletarian democracy, or any other social or economic system should be discussed, with all the attendant risks mentioned above, that some people might change their views. Assuming that one or the other of these ideas is

unacceptable, we can hardly rule it out in advance of a communal critical examination, and that examination will likely be an ongoing one. It would be a violation of academic freedom to disallow such discussion (or even advocacy) on or
off the campus, including courses.[22]

This discussion not only carries the inevitable risk that someone might change
his mind but also the risk of politicization in teaching and research, which currently appears to be a growing trend. As already noted, politicization has been
defined as "the practice of misstating or distorting or denying a truth or judgment
for which adequate grounds can be given, in behalf of a partisan political cause,
whether it be a revolutionary or a counterrevolutionary one."[23] So understood, the
practice of politicization (as distinguished from partisanship) clearly is not academically respectable. Attempts to regulate the practice, however, may run afoul
of the university's constitutional free speech provision and its marketplace of
ideas. Practitioners of politicization are hardly likely to admit to misstatement,
distortion, or denial of truths. On the contrary, they will claim, perhaps sincerely,
that the truth or warrant lies with them. The exposure of practitioners of politicization, like the exposure of fakes, frauds, and humbugs, therefore, has to pro-
ceed by argument. Moreover, the struggle against practitioners of politicization is
not only a struggle over ideas but, as has been said, also over facts.

Where do we stand on the issue of academic grounds for exclusion of an idea,
subject, or research program from the precincts of the university? Exclusion on
academic grounds is not a violation of the university's marketplace of ideas. And
if it can be shown that some idea or approach is riddled with falsehoods, that
would seem to be a legitimate reason for ruling it out. But the matter is not so
easy. For exponents of it are scarcely likely to agree that it is riddled with falsehoods. What we have to count on, then, is that critical examination in the marketplace of ideas will (in Holmesean fashion) *eventually* lead to its demise in the
community of scholars, the way so many ideas have passed away. That of course
is no guarantee of their falsity, and "dead" ideas are constantly being resurrected.
On the other side, universities are subject to "faddism," especially in the social
sciences and humanities. These fads die when interest in them is played out and
when new fads come along.

Moral–ideological arguments, on the other hand, seem to be an illegitimate
basis for exclusion, or at best a rather weak one. The fact that some set of hypotheses supports, or is believed to support, unacceptable moral–political conclusions
does not establish the hypotheses' invalidity. Such a result has to be demonstrated
by a communal critical examination; arguments have to be given, arguments that
have a foothold in the university community, because they are the sort recogniza-
ble as having force within the separate academic disciplines. Here, again, we have
to count on the operation of the marketplace of ideas to "debunk" them.[24]

Max Weinreich's words, written in 1946, are words of wisdom: "It makes all
the difference in the world whether a discussion is carried on in the cool atmosphere of specialized literature under a democracy that gives each side equal
opportunity of expression, or a controversial issue is made the basis of legislation
and administrative practice in a country ruled by an implacable dictatorship."[25]

Weinreich is talking about governmental control. Yet this thought is important for the university generally, in courses, student and faculty discussion groups, and its public arenas. As long there is an operating marketplace of ideas in which opponents of "unacceptable" ideas, as they see them, may express their views, there is less to fear from them than if only "acceptable" ideas were allowed.

THE ACADEMICIAN'S DILEMMA

Our conclusion in favor of an open marketplace of ideas in the university, however, may be said to raise the academician's dilemma. Suppose I believe that some subject, say, sociobiology or Marxist economics, is riddled with falsehoods. Because I might lack enough knowledge of the field to convince other people that that is the case, and because I believe in the free market of ideas, I might be inclined to not voice opposition to its having a place in the university. But suppose, also, I am a member of a curriculum committee that has to approve course proposals. How should I vote on the question? Though I would be hard pressed to vote in favor, I think I should probably do so, other things being equal, and would strongly suggest that its opponents mount a countercourse: at least I would want to be assured that the instructor will fairly discuss the criticisms of his or her approach. On the other hand, if I felt sufficiently capable of judging the subject for myself, I think I would vote against it, on what I take to be adequate academic grounds for rejecting it.

But suppose, also, that I believe that the subject of a course proposal supports political or moral conclusions that are unacceptable to me. Since I do not think that fact in itself shows the subject to be fundamentally or seriously flawed, I think I should have to vote for it, though I wouldn't be happy about it. There are in fact various courses around my own university in which I think such conclusions are taught, and I believe they have to be combated in the marketplace of ideas. Go one step further, however. If I *did* believe that the subject or the approach taken to it was fundamentally or seriously conceptually and methodologically flawed *and* that it was also presumed to support unacceptable political or moral conclusions, I should vote against it. For in that case, the subject would contain not only falsehoods but also *dangerous falsehoods*. I would also be worried about politicization.

Let me now summarize. We have gone through, in some detail, a sample argument about whether a subject may be kept out of the university on the grounds that it is not academically respectable. Keeping out such a subject is, it seems, compatible with the university's constitutional free speech provision. Yet, in each instance the case has to be made, not assumed. One sort of consideration, that the subject is conceptually and methodologically flawed, seems to me powerful. The second consideration, ideological flaw, seems to me to be weak. But our results are, in one respect, unexciting because the case has to be made *within* the gates of the university. That is where the debate has to take place, in the university's marketplace of ideas.[26]

We do of course pay a price for the university's marketplace of ideas. False-hoods and unacceptable ideas inevitably do get aired, and it is the job of the crit-ical community of scholars, operating in a marketplace of ideas, to expose them as such in order to advance knowledge. As Sylvester Stallone said on a related matter, "To express ourselves in good films, we also have to put up with the crap and violence and stupidity of the kind of films that are put out by guys who are pure exploiters."[27] And he oughta know.

Throughout the above exposition we spoke of "unacceptable" ideas and opin-ions. The term, however, was never defined. It was simply left to the reader to adopt his or her own definition or list of the term's denotation. We know what critics of sociobiology took to be *instances* of unacceptable ideas, but they gave no account of the meaning of the term or a standard for judging acceptability or unacceptability. As we turn again to speech codes, we shall see, I think, that it is not just maintained that some ideas or opinions are unacceptable but that attitudes are, as well.

NOTES

1. An instrumentalist rationale, it has been argued, makes the burden too easy to over-come, and a constitutive rationale is therefore endorsed. See chapter 2, n. 2.

2. *Schenck v. United States*, 249 U.S. 47, 52 (1919).

3. Alexander M. Bickel, *The Morality of Consent* (New Haven: Yale University Press, 1975), 72, 73, emphasis by Bickel. The quotation from Holmes is in his dissenting opin-ion in *Gitlow v. New York,* 268 U.S. 652, 673 (1925). Gitlow was convicted under a New York "criminal anarchy" statute that prohibited the "advocacy, advising or teaching the duty, necessity or propriety of overthrowing or overturning organized government by force or violence." My colleague, Professor William Van Alstyne, has suggested to me that, in the quoted sentence, Holmes is talking about the complex process of political discussion involved in amending the Constitution, whereby "the beliefs expressed in proletarian dic-tatorship" might be adopted.

4. Bickel, 76.

5. See Raphael Cohen-Almagor, "Why Tolerate? Reflections on the Millian Truth Prin-ciple," 25 *Philosophia* (1997), 131–52. Also see John Stuart Mill, *On Liberty* (Indianapo-lis, Ind.: Hackett, 1978), 9. Here, Mill maintains that "the only purpose for which power can be rightfully exercised over any member of a civilized community, against his will, is to prevent harm to others." He then goes on to argue for the utmost liberty of thought and expression in order to promote the truth. Cohen-Almagor argues that the Millian "harm principle" can come into conflict with the "truth principle."

6. See Mark Kingwell, "Is It Rational to Be Polite?," 90 *J. of Philosophy* (1993), 387–404.

7. On the debate, see M. Lippman, "The 1948 Convention on the Prevention and Pun-ishment of the Crime of Genocide: Forty-five Years Later," 8 *Temple Int'l & Comp. L.J.* (1994), 1–84.

8. Duke University, the university I am most familiar with, does not have a speech code but it does have freshman orientation, in which the "proper" messages are conveyed. Around 1990, some administrators promulgated "Duke Vision," which was presented in

orientation sessions by "facilitators" using techniques that approached "brainwashing." According to the Duke Vision: "Duke's image of a humane and just society is founded upon multiculural equality. . . . Racism and sexism are two common expressions of *uni-culturalism*. . . . They and other expressions of a worldview and value system based solely on any one culture are a denial of the humanity of others." What bothers many of the Vision's critics is its unabashed America bashing. See, generally, Fred Siegel, "The Cult of Multiculturalism," *New Republic*, February 18, 1991, 34–40. It is my understanding that the Duke Vision, as such, is no longer employed but its message is still conveyed.

9. Some orthodoxies or unquestioned theses may exist within a discipline because of ignorance of what has been established in another discipline or because of intellectual laziness, e.g., failure to check the originating sources of an idea. For interesting examples, see Richard F. Hamilton, *The Social Misconstruction of Reality: Validity and Verification in the Scholarly Community* (New Haven: Yale University Press, 1996).

10. *Doe v. University of Michigan*, 721 F. Supp. 852 (E.D. Mich. 1989). A vague code restriction is constitutionally defective because the individual is unable to predetermine whether his or her action will be legal (permitted) or illegal (prohibited). An overly broad restriction is defective because it regulates at least some protected activity or speech. For a discussion of *Doe,* see Timothy C. Shiell, *Campus Hate Speech on Trial* (Lawrence: University of Kansas Press, 1998), 74–78. See, also, appendix A.

11. It is not that courts never decide questions about courses. In 1985 a federal court invalidated a Louisiana law that required the teaching of creation science in public elementary and high schools on the grounds that the act violated the establishment clause of the First Amendment, because its purpose was to promote a religious belief. See *Aguillard v. Edwards*, 765 F.2d 1251 (1985); affirmed, *Edwards v. Aguillard*, 482 U.S. 578 (1987). ("Congress shall make no law respecting an establishment of religion, or prohibiting the free exercise thereof. . . .") I imagine that the result would have been the same had a public university been involved in the case.

12. 354 U.S. 234, 263 (1957). *Sweezy v. New Hampshire* is a central case in a line of cases establishing First Amendment status for academic freedom. See William W. Van Alstyne, "Academic Freedom and the First Amendment in the Supreme Court in the United States: An Unhurried Historical Review," 53 *Law and Contemporary Problems* (Summer 1990), 79–154.

13. To some extent the situation may be compared with the submission of an article to a scholarly journal. An article might be rejected for various reasons: too long, inappropriate for the particular journal, and poor quality. Rejection of article by a professional journal because of length, content, or quality is not a violation of the marketplace of ideas. (Of course, anything can be circulated on the Internet now.) In the last instance, that of quality, rejection is usually accompanied by the critical comments of reviewers. Generally, see David Shatz, "Is Peer Review Overrated?," 79 *The Monist* (1996), 536–63. Questions of quality cannot be avoided by the sort of argument criticized in chapter 2, at n. 20. See, also, chapter 2, n. 17.

14. See E. O. Wilson, "Science and Ideology," 8 *Academic Questions* (Summer 1995), 73–81. (Wilson is a leading figure in sociobiology.) Various groups were formed to combat sociobiology, e.g., the Ann Arbor Science for the People Collective. Going beyond this academic approach was the occasional disruption of lectures given by sociobiologists. Because of the opprobrium cast upon sociobiology, the field now goes under the name of evolutionary psychology. This field has researchers pursuing different lines, who may disagree among themselves, and who may have modified earlier claims. For purposes of our illustration, we shall consider the controversy as it stood before the name change.

15. Edward O. Wilson, *Sociobiology: A New Synthesis* (Cambridge, Mass.: Harvard University Press, 1975). For Wilson's later modifications, see C. J. Lumsden and E. O. Wilson, *Genes, Minds, and Culture: The Coevolutionary Process* (Cambridge, Mass.: Harvard University Press, 1981), advancing the idea of gene-culture coevolution and denying that genes (straightforwardly?) determine behavior. For an extensive bibliography and a detailed critique of Wilson and others, see Philip Kitcher, *Vaulting Ambition* (Cambridge, Mass.: MIT Press, 1985).

16. There is a distinction between sociobiology as a field of research for animals and humans and sociobiology as a set of particular theories and hypotheses. A showing that the latter set is flawed does not necessarily impugn the former. We shall not be concerned with the distinction here, since the attack on sociobiology appears to have been quite general.

17. See various articles in Arthur Caplan, ed., *The Sociobiology Debate* (New York: Harper & Row, 1978). For a more technical and not entirely dismissive treatment, see Kitcher, *Vaulting Ambition*.

18. Wilson, *Sociobiology*, 3.

19. Cited in Wilson, "Science and Ideology," 79, from a letter by the Sociobiology Study Group published in the *New York Review of Books* (November 13, 1975).

20. New York: Yiddish Scientific Institute-YIVO, 1946.

21. G. Kaplan and L. J. Rogers, "Race and Gender Fallacies: The Paucity of Biological Determinist Explanations of Difference," in Ethel Tobach and Betty Rosoff, eds., *Challenging Racism and Sexism: Alternatives to Genetic Explanations* (New York: Feminist Press at CUNY, 1994), at 76–77. See, also, the Ann Arbor Science for the People Collective, *Biology as a Social Weapon* (Minneapolis, Minn.: Burgess, 1977).

22. "A university is characterized by the spirit of free inquiry, its ideal being the ideal of Socrates—to follow the argument where it leads. . . . It is the business of a university to provide that atmosphere which is most conducive to speculation, experiment and creation." These two sentences appear in Frankfurter's concurring opinion in *Sweezy v. New Hampshire* (see n. 12) immediately before the statement of "the four essential freedoms of a university." In an investigative hearing conducted by the state Attorney General under the New Hampshire Subversive Activities Act, Paul Sweezy, a self-described "classical Marxist," refused to divulge what he had discussed in his lectures at the university. He was convicted of contempt, and according to Frankfurter Sweezy's academic freedom was violated.

23. Sidney Hook, "Intellectual Rot," *Measure* [UCRA], February 1989, 1.

24. This debunking is what opponents of sociobiology tried to achieve though the attempt was sometimes accompanied by disruptions that have no place in the university (see n. 14). If I can judge from the zoology and biology undergraduate students I have had in philosophy courses, the attempt has not been entirely successful.

25. *Hitler's Professors: The Part of Scholarship in Germany's Crimes against the Jewish People* (New York: Yiddish Scientific Institute-YIVO, 1946), 35.

26. Unfortunately, there are many courses given in universities and colleges that are not academically respectable, though in a sense somewhat different from that used here. These are courses that lack an adequate academic content or lack rigor. For this reason, constant scrutiny should be given to course offerings.

27. Cited in L. E. Ingelhart, *Press and Speech Freedoms in America, 1619–1995* (Westport, Conn.: Greenwood Press, 1997), 242.

Chapter Four

Campus Speech Restrictions I

VARIETIES OF SPEECH RESTRICTIONS

The campus speech code movement is declared by Samuel Walker to be the most successful American effort to restrict speech.[1] But Walker also suggests that the success was short-lived. He bases this judgment mainly on three court cases, two of them involving campus speech codes, and one, a city ordinance penalizing "hate" crimes.[2] The main constitutional defects found in the codes were vagueness (what does "stigmatizes or victimizes" mean?), overbreadth (reaching protected speech as well as some possibly unprotected speech), and violations of content- and viewpoint-neutrality (prohibiting some speech because of disagreement with its message). We shall not review these cases here.[3] Instead, we shall be looking at a series of articles that support speech codes. These articles give what I take to be the most powerful arguments, but I find them problematic nonetheless. We also, later, examine the Stanford University code, which is one of the most tightly formulated.

I think, though, that Walker's suggestion was hasty. The speech code cases dealt with public universities and left private institutions largely untouched. Moreover, as is often pointed out in the literature, even many public universities have kept their codes on the books.[4] It is of course difficult to tell how much they are enforced. Enforcement appears to take place sub rosa and students seem usually to submit to their sentences and do not challenge them in the courts. Anecdotal evidence indicates that this is also true of private campuses, and it probably is more extensive there. We only find out about the tip of the iceberg. We don't have much access to what the growing cohorts of deans, harassment coordinators, and facilitators do. Even more difficult to get at is the indoctrination in "right thinking" in freshman orientation and first-year writing courses, instances of which have been reported to me.

Campus "atmosphere" and the mere existence of a speech code, as we have seen, can have the effect of inhibiting free trade in ideas, by chilling the expression of unacceptable or unpopular thoughts. Atmosphere can deter taking up controversial or "touchy" topics, even in law school classes, where one would expect them.[5] In 1993, one university (Minnesota) went so far as to offer to provide students and instructors, on request, with a "campus climate adviser" who would be present in the classroom to oversee discussions of race, gender, and diversity, to ensure that they are respectful and not insulting.[6] Recall also the placing of a monitor in the classroom of Professor Gordon Snyder, referred to in chapter 1. Few people today are aware that in the 1960s members of the John Birch Society, a far-right group, tape-recorded professors' class lectures. Such actions clearly can have a intimidating effect on the expression, however respectful, of dissident or unpopular views.

Aside from speech codes, other speech-restricting devices are available. Many student activities receive funding through mandatory fees collected by a school, and they are dispersed to various groups by student councils and student governments. Some groups, however, may be highly benefited because their aims are favored, and others far less benefited because their aims are not favored. So, for example, there are instances of the defunding of dissident, usually conservative, student newspapers or organizations. At one time it was the defunding or deprivation of official recognition of radical, leftist groups such as the Students for a Democratic Society, the notorious SDS.[7] In contrast to such "nonofficial" speech restrictions as theft of newspapers and tearing down posters, these have a kind of official status.

University and college administrations have also moved against student publications and groups that are critical of them. Posters, flyers, and skits (admittedly often in bad taste: see example 15, in chapter 1) that make fun of administration policies, but which arguably are expressions of ideas, have been ordered removed by administrations in knee-jerk reactions. Some of these policies concern such contentious topics as race, gender, and multiculturalism. The president of George Washington University stated that, while he supported freedom of the press, it was wrong to use student tuition dollars "to print newspapers that offend us."[8] So much for the vaunted importance of diversity, at least as far as diversity of ideas goes.[9]

PRELIMINARIES ON SPEECH CODES

We now have to examine arguments for speech codes and other such expression-restricting devices more directly, particularly, though not exclusively, as they might affect students. We shall focus on a group of writers, Critical Race Theorists, who make a powerful case for campus as well as noncampus speech restrictions. If their case does not succeed, it is not likely that any other case will.

But we should begin by agreeing on one thing: a "zero tolerance" code, a code that would prohibit *anything* that *anyone* finds offensive, is clearly unacceptable.

It would make campus life unbearable were it strictly enforced; it would prevent the discussion of any topic that might be "unwelcome" to any individual. And it's not just that people would have to think before they speak—ordinarily not a bad thing. In fact, though, such a code would not be uniformly enforced; certain occasions of speech would be punished and others not (often for ideological reasons), which is plainly unfair. Second, "merely offensive" expressions shouldn't be speech code violations. Such a rule would clearly be too restrictive and would contravene the university's own constitutional free speech provision, let alone the First Amendment.[10] And it probably won't help to say that "very offensive" speech should be prohibited. Burning the American flag in protest is very offensive to very many people but few defenders (faculty and students) of speech restrictions would want it to be a crime. To ask, then, what degree or kind of offensiveness one wants to prevent, requires that one consider *why* some forms of speech should be interdicted and others not.

And it is not just speech codes as such that are at issue. Some campuses do not have a code that is explicitly called a speech code. For example, Duke University prides itself on not having a speech code. But virtually all campuses have conduct codes, as student handbooks show, and these generally forbid *harassing* behavior, under which "verbal harassment" may be subject to punishment. This applies to faculty and other employees as well. For instance, Duke University does have a harassment code, discussed later, which can substitute for a speech code, though Duke is pretty solicitous of the freedom of speech. When we speak of speech codes here, we mean to cover harassment codes that impinge on speech as well.

Speech codes vary in their details, with too much variety to list here. The University of Michigan code covered classroom expressions while the University of Wisconsin code explicitly exempted the classroom, and it was also not applicable to faculty, which has its own code.[11] Some codes require that the proscribed language be used "intentionally," others allow for "strict liability." According to the University of Maryland–College Park, "idle chatter of a sexual nature" is an unacceptable verbal behavior. (One wonders what the talk is like in locker rooms—only serious chatter, perhaps.) As noted, most, perhaps all, campus codes forbid "harassment," which may include "sexually suggestive staring, leering, sounds, or gestures," as well as "heterosexist remarks or jokes" (Syracuse University).[12]

How did we get to this situation? Commentators have found it puzzling. On many college campuses the doctrine of in loco parentis, that the university stands in place of the parent, had gone moribund in the aftermath of the student unrest of the late 1960s. The idea that the university should exercise moral authority over students became a nonstarter. But the codes seem to have revived it in some degree. As far as I am aware, no academic institution has put a restrictive speech code to a vote to see if students feel the need to be protected. It would take us too far afield to speculate on how this revival came about.[13] What we can do is look at some academic writing that directly or indirectly lends support to campus speech restrictions and also the influence of federal legislation on harassment in the workplace.

The writers we shall examine want to contextualize the First Amendment and to some extent I find this aspect of their thought congenial. I believe that the law should be interpreted and applied in a fact-sensitive way, that courts should take into account the social consequences of their decisions, and that interests have to be balanced. I think this is especially true with respect to the judicially developed common law, though too much fact-sensitivity can lead to the erosion of legal rules and principles. Nevertheless, I think that the case for contextualization is harder to make regarding the civil liberties enshrined in the Bill of Rights, and especially the liberties in the First Amendment. Only the most compelling case should allow us to intrude on these liberties. And because the freedom of speech is so vital to the work of universities, the same holds for the free speech provision of the university's constitution. In fact, the freedom of speech is so central to the activity of the university, the pursuit of knowledge, that it may be more important there than in society generally.

WORDS THAT WOUND

We earlier noted two main, and interrelated, motivations for campus speech restrictions: promotion of a "comfortable learning environment" and protection from "verbal behavior" that may cause hurt. Students need to be protected from demeaning and denigrating speech if they are to be—and feel—equal on campus. Furthermore, punishing "hate speech" teaches people that racism or other prejudice is unacceptable and can bring about tolerance and sensitivity. It is also said, depending on how a code is formulated, that no legitimate campus speech is in fact prohibited.

On the other side, there is the objection, as a matter of principle, that a university has no business determining which ideas or expressions are acceptable and which groups or individuals deserve protection by limiting the speech of others; moreover, that speech codes suffer from difficulties in formulation in that they are vague and overly broad; and finally, that they allow too much discretion to those charged with their administration. All these points, pro and con, raise contentious matters.

Perhaps the most important academic writing in favor of speech restrictions, and not just in campus codes, comes from Critical Race Theory, written by authors of Asian, African American, and Chicano descent, whose articles are reprinted in an important collection, *Words That Wound*.[14] These articles make a powerful case for campus speech restrictions. Their focus often tends to be narrow, that is, on race. As stated earlier, if their case does not succeed, it is not likely that any other case will. So, their arguments, which I present in some detail, merit careful examination. Their positions on campus speech are embedded in more general considerations about speech.

Drawing on the social sciences and their own life experience as minorities, the critical race theorists want to "contextualize" First Amendment jurisprudence, which they otherwise regard as "absolutist" and "extremist." They want to abandon the liberal pretense of "neutrality," and to openly endorse a value-laden approach. Consider, for example, state and local laws that prohibit parading in masks or hoods. Everyone knows that these laws are aimed at the Ku Klux Klan. Why not be honest about it? A law specifically prohibiting only Klansmen probably would fail the test of viewpoint-neutrality; the law would be aimed at the Klan's message.

While the issue of the compatibility of campus speech restrictions with the U.S. Constitution is not of prime importance to us, as such, we do have to deal with the critical race theorists' approach to it because matters of principle are raised. Most important is the fact that these writers want us to look at offensive speech from the point of view of the recipient, the victim. This idea is expressed in the very title of Professor Mari Matsuda's article, "Public Response to Racist Speech: Considering the Victim's Story." [15]

The "critical" approach has an antecedent in the call for the repression of American Nazis and their propaganda in the 1930s. Here too there was opposition to the "exaggerated formalism of the rule of law." [16] Most prominent was the distinguished sociologist-lawyer David Riesman. In line with the legal realism of his day, Riesman argued for a sociological, contextualized jurisprudence. In other terms, he wanted the law, including free speech law, to be sensitive to the facts. Words have different meanings and effects, depending on time, place, speaker, and audience. Calling a political candidate an anti-Semite in New York, he maintained, would be "clearly devastating" and therefore defamatory, but that would not necessarily be true somewhere else. [17]

The "words that wound" concept of the critical race theorists goes beyond Riesman's argument. Their position is strongly in line with the motivations we've discussed for campus speech restrictions. These writers begin by pointing to the numerous racial affronts experienced by blacks in recent years.

INSULT AS ASSAULT

Although Richard Delgado is not primarily concerned with campus speech, he introduces some influential ideas to the "critical race theory" position on codes. [18] He focuses, in particular, on the harm caused by racist speech. While it hardly needs demonstration that racial insults are detestable, Professor Delgado maintains that a racial insult is a kind of assault and that restriction of racist speech can pass constitutional muster under the First Amendment. [19] Delgado argues that the traditional torts (legally actionable civil wrongs) of defamation and intentional infliction of emotional distress are inadequate to deal with hate speech, particularly that directed against blacks. Only in passing does he take note of epithets and slurs directed against other groups.

Delgado surveys the social science literature on the psychologically damaging effects of verbal racism and argues for an "action for racial insult," an independent tort for racial slurs. Racial insults are qualitatively different from mere insults because they "conjure up the entire history of racial discrimination in this country." [20] The racial insult is a kind of assault, a verbal slap in the face, as some

writers have put it. Second, Delgado argues that a tort for racial insult can overcome constitutional free speech objections. Racial insults are not very different
from other kinds of speech that may be constitutionally restricted, such as obscen-
ities and "fighting words." A racial insult, unlike the slogan in *Cohen* ("Fuck the
Draft"), is not political speech; "its perpetrator intends not to discover truth or
advocate social action."[21] As an assault, racist speech approaches a physical blow,
which is subject to restriction by the law. Delgado's points are expanded by other
critical race theorists.

Delgado, then, apparently maintains that the racial insult is "non-speech," not
really speech at all, not the expression of an idea. Another possibility, which is
suggested by the comparison with fighting words, is that he regards it as "low-
value" speech that could, under certain conditions, be subject to punitive sanctions.[22] The characterization of some speech as low value, however, may depend
on a value judgment about its substantive message. Obscenity is sometimes said
to be "no-value" speech.

Professor Delgado's argument is applicable to campus speech: racial slurs are
subject to restriction and discipline in campus codes. Quite obviously, he maintains that such insults are not "merely offensive." They are words that cause substantial harm to their recipients. It is in any case significant that for Delgado the
distinctive quality of the insult is its *racial* component understood in a particular
way. "You dumb honkey" directed to a white would be legally actionable only in
the "unusual situation" where the recipient suffers substantial harm. (A better
example might be "You dumb racist." Probably little is more wounding to a white
liberal than to be called a racist, although for some it has a redemptive effect.) On
the other hand, "You damn nigger," said by a white, would almost always be
actionable, and damages could be awarded presumably even in the absence of
harm to the recipient in order to deter speech insulting to blacks, according to
Delgado.[23] Although campus speech codes are not about instituting a special tort
action, slurs directed to black students similarly may be proscribed in campus
speech codes and be subject to disciplinary action.[24]

I find myself torn by Professor Delgado's position, not so much by his argument itself, but because I think that racial and ethnic slurs deliberately directed
against *any* group are vile, loathsome, and morally contemptible. I am not a moral
relativist. Yet his approach gives rise to a number of questions that trouble me.
These questions also arise regarding other critical race theorists. We shall therefore consider some of them here, keeping in mind that they apply to other writers.

SOME QUESTIONS ON DELGADO'S APPROACH

Delgado's article deals almost entirely with single *words,* epithets and slurs, and
his position rests on an empirical claim about the psychologically damaging
effects of racial insults and their symbolic nature, that they "conjure up the entire
history of racial discrimination in this country." How would "other groups" fare
on this analysis? And what about ideas that demean? Are these tortious too? Or

are expressions of demeaning ideas speech that is protected by the First Amendment?[25] Let us consider an example involving a different group.

American Jews experience the smearing of swastikas on synagogues as offensive and outrageous. Such acts are punishable as vandalism, but Jews are highly troubled by them, given the history of anti-Semitism in the United States and elsewhere. Admittedly, anti-Semitism has declined in America, though it continues to surface, even in universities. The symbolic meaning of the swastika is too obvious to need an explanation. In 1977 there began a year-long controversy over whether a neo-Nazi group, the National Socialist Party of America, could hold a march through the Village of Skokie, a suburb of Chicago where many Holocaust survivors lived. At one point the American Jewish Congress argued for prohibiting only the display of the swastika as a "deliberately provocative and abusive symbol." Others stressed that the demonstration itself would inflict "psychic trauma" on the Holocaust survivors.[26]

It seems, then, that other groups may also have a plausible claim for a tort of racial assault or some similar dignitary or civility tort. Thus, displays of swastikas arguably should be assaults for which Jews who experience distress ought to receive compensation. Granted, blacks have suffered from a long history of racial discrimination, as Delgado says. However, once a claim for racial assault, by the display of a hateful word or symbol, is recognized, other groups are sure to stand in line with an equally good, or nearly equally good, claim as a result of the fact-sensitive contextualization of the First Amendment. One very reputable writer, whose name I won't mention, thinks that blacks experience greater suffering from an insult than members of religious groups. This empirical claim is at least debatable. It should not be forgotten that Jews have been castigated as a "race"—recall German "racial science."[27] And the brunt of anti-Semitism is not that Jews merely are an "inferior" race but something worse: that they are "evil." Even the word "Jew" often has a derogatory connotation. In any case, the Holocaust survivors in Skokie would have experienced severe psychic stress from the display of swastikas in a neo-Nazi march.

Now it should be noticed that the elements of the cause of action for racial insult (see n. 23) are not formulated with reference to a particular race; yet Delgado's entire argument turns on the uniqueness of the black experience and fails, therefore, to support his general proposal. On the other hand, to confine the concept of assault by insult to blacks seems too narrow. Surely, other groups would complain that they are being unfairly left out, whether in a civil action or in a campus speech code. But where do we draw the line? May other groups claim "victim" status? (See the discussion, below, of Professor Matsuda.) Extending assault by insult to other groups contains a major difficulty, namely, the evaluation of the evidence on the psychologically damaging effects of verbal assault against this or that group. Such a task is beyond the competence of courts.

And it is also beyond the competence of university administrators who have instituted speech codes that prohibit speech that purportedly denigrates students on the basis of their race, religion, sexual orientation, Vietnam veteran status, HIV status, political affiliation, pregnancy status, etc. These codes come close to a "zero tolerance" code. I would question how much these designations have depended on an evaluation of evidence of psychological harm. Rather, I think that it is political ideology and administrators' fear of lawsuits that are at work. The "victim industry" has also had an impact.

Even more difficult, and problematic for campus speech, than insults are "sanitized" racism and anti-Semitism, that is, racism and anti-Semitism presented as "scholarship." College courses that promote sanitized racism and anti-Semitism tend to be highly "politicized," in the sense used earlier, and as such are academically questionable.[28] Holocaust denial is a case in point: for Jews it "conjures up the entire history of anti-Semitism," to use Delgado's phrase.[29] Also very highly troubling to Jews are anti-Semitic expressions by such black figures as Minister Louis Farrakhan (Judaism is a "gutter religion") and Khallid Muhummad, inflammatory and exaggerated claims about Jewish involvement in the slave trade, claims about the responsibility of Jews for AIDS among blacks, and the distribution of *The Protocols of the Elders of Zion* at meetings of some black student groups in universities.[30] All these are, of course, expressions of ideas, which in fact are potentially more damaging than the isolated epithet, slur, or insult. These ideas may stimulate actions that have disastrous consequences. The same is true of "scholarly" claims about the alleged intellectual inferiority of blacks and the gross sexuality of black males. But shall expression of such ideas be actionable, on Delgado's approach?

Probably not. For as Delgado apparently holds, the racial epithet is invoked as an assault, not as a statement of fact that may be proven true or false. And if this is correct, utterance of a racial epithet in the logically appropriate context is arguably not an expression of an idea, and so arguably is not protected by the First Amendment. Ideas, "sanitized racism," on the other hand, even if detestable, are protected speech, he may hold. But should they be, once the liberal pretense of "neutrality" is abandoned and the First Amendment is "contextualized," which David Riesman had already argued for in the 1930s? If one wants to penalize "wounding words" it makes no sense to single out gutter epithets, as the African American academic Henry Louis Gates Jr., says.[31]

And there is another issue. Is it the case that epithets or slurs have no intellectual content, do not convey ideas? The display of the Confederate flag may be just as offensive to blacks as the swastika is to Jews, and isn't this so because of what these objects *symbolize*, the messages or ideas that they convey? And doesn't the use of such emotive terms as "nigger" and "kike" convey a message? Of course, it is often difficult to tell what the message is or to disentangle the cognitive component from the emotive. The epithet/idea distinction is not easy to make; ideas and beliefs are central to most slurs. For example, the imperative sentence, "Get away from me you dirty nigger [kike]," cannot be true or false, but it does probably connote the speaker's belief that blacks [Jews] are inferior to him. Moreover, it seems wrong to say that an advocate of racial and religious tolerance, such as Delgado, may use such words, but an opponent may not.

Because epithets and slurs can have an intellectual or ideational component, penalizing their use may have the effect of suppressing the expression of ideas.

This conclusion, however, makes me uneasy because I do not think that racial, ethnic, or religious slurs have a place on the college campus, which is committed to rational thinking, especially in the classroom. But punishment is something else. I believe that the overwhelming majority of members of the academic community, faculty and students, don't like vilifiers; their nasty words make us angry and to want to punish the user. A punitive approach, however, forces us—and the courts—to take sides on whose speech is palatable. In particular, it also creates an atmosphere in which people hesitate to express controversial ideas, and not just on matters of race. It doesn't please me that "sanitized" racism and anti-Semitism, which can be more damaging than slurs, should not be punishable; these, however, have to be countered by argument. In any case, if Delgado doesn't think so, other critical race theorists do seem to allow that demeaning ideas could be suppressed. Let us turn then to another critical race theory writer.

THE RACIAL INSULT AS A MESSAGE OF SUBORDINATION

Charles Lawrence, a black law professor at Stanford University, takes Delgado one step further. Lawrence maintains that campus regulations that prohibit face-to-face vilification and protect captive audiences (e.g., students living in a dorm) from spoken and written harassment can be defended within the confines of existing First Amendment doctrine. What is more, he suggests that the Constitution may in fact *mandate* restrictions on some racial speech. He also deals directly with the college campus. His argument is important for us because he wants to cover the cases of both private and public institutions.

An occurrence at Stanford University is described in the introduction to the collection, *Words That Wound*: "Two white freshmen had defaced a poster bearing the likeness of Beethoven. They had colored the drawing of Beethoven brown, given it wild curly hair, big lips, and red eyes, posted it on the door of an African-American student's dorm room in Ujamaa, the Black theme house. The two white students involved had been in an argument with the Black student the night before. They had contested the Black student's assertion that Beethoven was of African descent." The general attitude on the Stanford campus was that this was an unrepresentative prank, and at any rate the students could not be disciplined under then existing university rules.

Lawrence experienced this incident differently; he experienced it as a blow. The injury was not only to the particular black student, but also to him. And not just to him. It was an injury to the members of a *group*. To put it slightly differently, he experienced an injury because of his membership in a particular group, even though the poster was not specifically directed at him. The Ujamaa incident gave rise to his article, "If He Hollers Let Him Go: Regulating Racist Speech on Campus."[32] Lawrence does not hang his approach on the 1952 Supreme Court decision upholding an Illinois group libel statute, as many others have done.[33] Rather, Lawrence advances the ingenious argument that the 1954 *Brown v. Board of Education* desegregation decision should be viewed as a *speech* case.

What *Brown* declared to be unconstitutional (on Fourteenth Amendment equal protection grounds) was not merely state-enforced separation of blacks and whites in public schools. That was bad enough. Rather, Lawrence argues, the underlying fault was the *message* of the inferiority of blacks that segregation conveyed, an assault on their entitlement to equal dignity.[34] As the Court said, segregated schools stigmatized blacks with a badge of inferiority. *Brown*, Lawrence therefore suggests, may be read as regulating the *content* of racist speech. The idea of racial inferiority is inseparable from the practice of segregation. And it is also inseparable from racially insulting speech. *Brown*, he says, "reflects the understanding that racism is a form of subordination that achieves its purposes through group defamation."[35] (Lawrence's approach, as well as that of other critical race theorists, tracks the feminist argument that pornography is a form of sex discrimination prohibited by the Fourteenth Amendment.[36]) A question that one might ask here is whether banishing racist speech banishes subordination.

Now, it is standard doctrine that regulation of speech generally must be content-neutral. Thus, time, place, and manner restrictions are allowable, but not restrictions that fall outside of such recognized exceptions as obscenity, solicitation to commit a crime, and so on. Lawrence expresses his concern to defend unpopular ideas against the tyranny of the majority. On his view, however, racist speech is a special evil, for it assaults the dignity of the individual and causes feelings of inferiority and unworthiness. The civil libertarians who defend racist speech have not listened to its real victims.

In the course of developing his argument, Lawrence takes up various objections, among them that he has conflated the public/private distinction. The import of the public/private distinction is that there are all sorts of matters that belong in the realm of the private and personal choice and decision of the individual, and are outside the control or intervention of the government. If the use of contraceptive devices by a married couple falls within the zone of privacy, even more so do the private individual's messages protected by the First Amendment. The *Brown* decision, on which Lawrence relies so much, applied to "state action" of enforced segregation and not to any private person's discriminatory message of racial inferiority.

To this objection Lawrence offers an interesting response. The objection views privacy in the abstract and ignores the way it operates in the real world; it views privacy as something in which we all have an equal stake. The fact is that privacy in its various forms, in speech and personal decision, exists only because of state action, that is, the protections afforded to them by the state.

Now, the public/private distinction can be problematic in some circumstances, but in this attempt to break it down there lurks a danger; it can easily take us down the proverbial "slippery slope" and undermine the individual's freedoms. For on Lawrence's approach virtually anything can be viewed as "state action," so nothing is potentially immune from governmental intrusion.[37]

Here we see the significance of regarding the racist message as a special evil. Lawrence does accord value to individual privacy and personal choice. But he insists that the inequities have to be weighed in the balance. There is, he says, "some point at which the balance ought to be struck in its [privacy's] favor *after full consideration of the inequities that might accompany that choice*."[38] What he objects to is privacy language that ignores inequities and assumes we all share equally in the value being promoted. Privacy should not be regarded in the abstract but in context. Sometimes we have to rule against privacy.

These claims are followed by a curious example. The Supreme Court has recognized a woman's right to terminate a pregnancy, yet the Court has also held that there is no constitutional right entitling her to financial resources to have an abortion. The right to terminate a pregnancy, then, is not of equal value to everyone. This is correct, but what follows from it? Does my right to drive a car entail an entitlement to be supplied with gasoline? Surely not.

Yet it is true that some particular rights and liberties are not of equal value to everyone, in the sense that not everyone can take advantage of them. So the inequities have to be put on the balancing scale. The right of privacy (freedom of speech, in this context), it is being claimed, is not of the same value to blacks as it is to members of other groups. (But what would have happened to the black civil rights movement without freedom of speech?) And given that racist speech is a special evil, the need to protect blacks from the harm of racist speech overbalances the need to protect racist speech that stops short of physical violence.

Lawrence's approach, thus far, seems to me to have some power, because courts do have to weigh and balance interests and rights. In particular, I would agree that the extravagantly abstract notion of a right of privacy has gotten way out of hand. The Constitution, though, puts its finger on the scale in favor of the freedom of speech, and I find Lawrence's interpretation of *Brown* as a speech (defamation) case rather debatable. Furthermore, while it may be argued that the *state* is, or should be, required to respect the citizen's entitlement to equal dignity, it is far from clear to me that any individual is, or should be, *legally* required to respect it (though morality may require such respect). Similarly, the administrations of public colleges and universities perhaps, if Lawrence's argument is sound, legally ought to respect a student's entitlement to equal dignity, by controlling their own speech. But requiring that students respect it under pain of punishment is more dubious. Here we have a conflict between equality and individual liberty. And as Henry Louis Gates remarks, "to suggest that equality must precede liberty is to jettison the latter without securing the former."[39] The proper avenue for achieving this respect is through education (in my opinion, particularly by the study of Western thought), which should also teach students to respect the expression of ideas they disagree with and to counter them with argument. The solution is neither a speech code nor "sensitivity" training. Respect for the *expression* of ideas one disagrees with does not mean that one necessarily respects those ideas or that silence or acquiescence is required. Sometimes, even ridicule is appropriate.[40]

In any event, we are left with all the questions that arose in connection with Delgado, and even more so because Lawrence is explicitly concerned with the *message* of racism. Since that is the case, we should be concerned with much more than epithets and slurs, but also with expressions of racist ideas, which are worse invasions of dignity. Lawrence avers that he doesn't want to restrict all racist speech but his argument gives us no place to draw the line.

THE STANFORD POLICY

Lawrence's defense of the Stanford speech code, however, does suggest a line with respect to the campus, perhaps because he thinks it should be a hospitable place. He endorses its "fighting words" approach, though he would like to have had added to it the notion that hate speech that occurs in settings where there is a "captive audience" may be regulated. The Stanford policy, Lawrence argues, can pass muster under current constitutional doctrines. Stanford is a private institution, and one might think that it need not conform to constitutional speech protections.[41] But like those of many universities, the code proclaims its acceptance of principles of free inquiry and free expression, and Lawrence apparently wants his argument to have application to academic institutions generally, public and private. The fighting words approach derives from the 1942 case of *Chaplinsky v. New Hampshire* (315 U.S. 568). Lawrence maintains that racist abuse is a variety of, or "functionally equivalent" to, the *Chaplinsky* doctrine.[42]

Most people today know the Jehovah's Witnesses as polite individuals who hand out religious literature on the street corner or at the front door, but some years ago they conducted their proselytizing in a more aggressive manner. In the course of his public proselytizing in Rochester, New Hampshire, Chaplinsky, a Witness, denounced organized religion, especially the Roman Catholic Church, and a disturbance ensued. A police officer conducted Chaplinsky to the police station, without arresting him. While en route Chaplinsky encountered the city marshal who had earlier admonished him to "go slow." They had an exchange of words, and Chaplinsky said to the marshal: "You are a God damned racketeer" and "a damned Fascist and the whole government of Rochester are Fascists or agents of Fascists." He was convicted of violating a state statute that forbids anyone to address "any offensive, derisive or annoying word to any other person who is lawfully in any street or other public place" or "call him by any offensive or derisive name."

The Supreme Court, per Justice Frank Murphy, upheld the conviction:

> There are certain well-defined and narrowly limited classes of speech, the prevention and punishment of which have never been thought to raise any Constitutional problem. These include the lewd and obscene, the profane, the libelous, and the insulting or "fighting" words—those which by their very utterance inflict injury or tend to incite an immediate breach of the peace. *It has been well observed that such utterances are no essential part of any exposition of ideas, and are of such slight social value as a step to truth that any benefit that may be derived from them is clearly outweighed by the social interest in order and morality.*

Citing the state court's interpretation of the statute, Justice Murphy goes on to say that no words were forbidden "except such as have a direct tendency to cause acts of violence by the persons to whom, individually, the remark is addressed. . . . The statute, as construed, does no more than prohibit the face-to-face words plainly likely to cause a breach of the peace by the addressee."[43] The Court, in 1942 at least, thought it obvious that "damned racketeer" and "damned Fascist" are epithets likely to provoke the average person to retaliation. It is generally understood that the part of Murphy's statement, "those [words] which by their very utterance inflict injury," is nugatory.

The words we have emphasized in Murphy's statement are highly significant for any consideration of the limits of campus speech. Face-to-face fighting words do not contribute to the university's goal of the promotion of knowledge.

The Stanford speech policy ("Fundamental Standard Interpretation: Free Expression and Discriminatory Harassment") is recognized as one of the most carefully drafted of all such campus codes.[44] It therefore is worth examining, even though it has been struck down by a California court. Let us see how well it tracks *Chaplinsky*. The Interpretation's essentials are as follows:

1. Stanford is committed to the principles of free inquiry and free expression. Students have the right to hold and vigorously defend and promote their opinions. . . . Respect for this right requires that students tolerate even expression of opinions which they find abhorrent. . . .

2. Stanford is also committed to principles of equal opportunity and non-discrimination. Each student has the right of equal access to a Stanford education, without discrimination on the basis of sex, race, color, handicap, religion, sexual orientation, or national and ethnic origin. Harassment of students on the basis of any of these characteristics contributes to a hostile environment that makes access to education for those subjected to it less than equal. Such discriminatory harassment is therefore considered to be a violation of the Fundamental Standard.

3. This interpretation of the Fundamental Standard is intended to clarify the point at which protected free expression ends and prohibited discriminatory harassment begins. Prohibited harassment includes discriminatory intimidation by threats of violence, and also includes personal vilification of students on the basis of their sex, race, color, handicap, religion, sexual orientation, or national and ethnic origin.

4. Speech or other expression constitutes harassment by vilification if it:

(a) is intended to insult or stigmatize an individual or a small number of individuals on the basis of their sex, race, color, handicap, religion, sexual orientation, or national and ethnic origin; and

(b) is addressed directly to the individual or individuals whom it insults or stigmatizes; and

(c) makes use of "fighting" words or non-verbal symbols.

In the context of discriminatory harassment, "fighting" words or non-verbal symbols are words, pictures, or symbols that, by virtue of their form, are commonly understood to convey direct and visceral hatred or contempt for human beings on the basis of their sex, race, color, handicap, religion, sexual orientation, or national and ethnic origin.

It is important to notice that the elements (a), (b), and (c) are jointly necessary for the campus offense of harassment by vilification.

This regulation, I think, overlaps with *Chaplinsky*, but it also adds to and sub-tracts from it. It overlaps, because it too requires "face-to-face" use of fighting words. It adds, because it requires that the insult be on the basis of sex, race, color, etc., which is entirely absent from the case. And it subtracts, because it does not require that the fighting words be likely to provoke the average person to retaliation, but rather that they convey "direct and visceral hatred or contempt." One is left to wonder why Stanford doesn't simply prohibit any harassment by the use of words that convey "direct and visceral hatred or contempt" directed face-to-face at *any* student. Isn't that bad enough? So, too, for intimidation by threats of violence. Why "discriminatory intimidation" by threats of violence? The pro-liferation of anonymous threats is a disturbing campus phenomenon today. Per-haps, though, all these are prohibited by the "Fundamental Standard" itself. If so, however, the above harassment code seems superfluous. Why, then, *discrimina-tory* harassment as a separate violation?

Professor Thomas C. Grey, the architect of the Stanford policy, answers this question very much in terms given by Delgado and Lawrence:

> Obviously, it is University policy not to discriminate against *any* student in the administration of its educational policies on *any* arbitrary or unjust basis. Why then enumerate "sex, race, color, handicap, religion, sexual orientation, and national and ethnic origin" as specially prohibited bases for discrimination? The reason is that, in this society at this time, these characteristics tend to make individuals possessing them the target of socially pervasive invidious discrimination. . . . In addition, for most of these groups, a long history associates extreme verbal abuse with intimida-tion by physical violence, so that vilification is experienced as assaultive in the strict sense. It is the cumulative and socially pervasive discrimination, often linked to vio-lence, that distinguishes the intolerable injury of *wounded identity* caused by dis-criminatory harassment from the tolerable, and relatively randomly distributed, hurt of bruised feelings that results from single incidents of ordinary personally motivated name-calling, a form of hurt that we do not believe the Fundamental Standard pro-tects against.[45]

There is much to comment on in this reply, some of which is contained in our remarks on Delgado and Lawrence. In any case, it is clear that the code wants to make a statement, as is evident from provision (2). While Stanford asserts a com-mitment to principles of free inquiry and free expression, provision (1), it finds it wanting when put in the balance and weighed against its commitment to princi-ples of equal opportunity and nondiscrimination. So it is not enough to outlaw harassment alone; it is "discriminatory harassment" that must be outlawed. In so doing, the Stanford code goes beyond *Chaplinsky*, which says nothing about dis-criminatory harassment. In fact, it appears to be adopting language from federal law on workplace harassment, which we look at later. Meanwhile, I wonder how much it prevents "wounded identity."[46] In fact, I believe, discriminatory harass-ment codes promote the resentment of groups not covered by them.

The Stanford code is tightly drafted, and it represents a noble effort on Professor Grey's part to protect campus speech to the extent it is compatible with the aim of eliminating discriminatory harassment. The code is *almost*, but not quite, acceptable to me. For even a tightly drafted code can have a chilling effect on speech.

Part of the reason I do not find it entirely acceptable is expressed in the Duke University Law School's "Rules, Policies, and Procedures":

> When students have allowed standards of civility to slip seriously in ways repeatedly hurtful to others entitled to share the campus equally with themselves the response at some universities to such recurrently offensive activities has been more rules. Such requests have been made to us to make more rules, but this is not an undertaking welcomed by us [the law school's administration] or by the faculty. We want you to know why this is so.
>
> Regulation of student expression, whether of particular viewpoints, or even of the circumstances or manner of their utterance, is a very tricky undertaking. Such rules often convey their own intolerance without meaning to do so. However artfully drawn, they can chill a good deal of provocative expression that is altogether desirable, especially within a lively professional school. They also convey the message that those who carry unpopular messages are being told to be quiet. The business to "judicialize" academic life and our relationships is often also a sign of mutual failure to operate within the common sense notions discussed earlier [good judgment, self-restraint, and civility].[47]

The crucial sentences occur in the second paragraph: "Such rules often convey their own intolerance without meaning to do so. However artfully drawn, they can chill a good deal of provocative expression that is altogether desirable. . . ."

It seems to me that a prohibition on some forms of racist or sexist speech may easily be seen as a general viewpoint-based restriction; certain speech is condoned and other speech is proscribed. It conveys the broader message that speech that doesn't fit in with the official, underlying viewpoint is better not spoken.

Aside from this general concern, to which I shall return, there are other difficulties. Exactly what does Stanford's phrase (4c), "commonly understood to convey direct and visceral hatred or contempt for human beings on the basis of their sex, race," etc., cover? Would a black calling a white a racist offend against the code? Or is this an instance of "victim's privilege"? (See the discussion of Professor Matsuda, in chapter 5.)

Consider the infamous "water buffalo" affair at the University of Pennsylvania, which stretched out over a number of months. On the night of January 13, 1993, a group of women from a black sorority were very loudly singing, chanting, and stomping under Eden Jacobowitz's dormitory window. He was working on a paper for a course. Jacobowitz shouted out, "Please be quiet." The noise continued and he shouted out, "Shut up, you water buffalo." Jacobowitz was then charged with a violation of Penn's policy on racial harassment. While Penn's policy is not identical to Stanford's, it is close to it. Our question is whether Stanford's provision covers this case. It shouldn't, but one doesn't really know.[48]

The Stanford policy is not problem free for people unfairly *charged* with the offense of discriminatory harassment by vilification. There are numerous reports of people, students and faculty, who have been perceived to vilify or harass someone and who were, as a result, put through the wringer. Sometimes they were vindicated in the end, but often the proceedings ended inconclusively, and they ended up being stigmatized as racists, sexists, and so on.[49] Perhaps even more than in the public realm, merely being accused of a "speech offense" on campus can be quite serious.

A good noncampus example of the problem occurred in January 1999 in Washington, D.C. David Howard, the mayoral ombudsman, who is white, said the following at a budget meeting with two coworkers, one of whom was black: "I will have to be niggardly with this fund because it's not going to be a lot of money." The black coworker became incensed; Howard apologized and submitted his resignation, which was quickly accepted by the mayor. The word "niggardly," however, has no connection to the racial slur, which entered English about 1700, from the Latin "niger," or "black." According to etymologists the word "niggardly" goes back to the fourteenth-century Scandinavian term "niggard," meaning "miser," and some speculate that it goes back earlier to a Middle English word. Howard said that he learned the word for his S.A.T. test in high school. His problem was that the word *sounded* like the slur.[50] The indignation industry seems to have been at work here, and many people thought that the mayor did right to accept Howard's resignation immediately rather than rise to his defense; Howard should have watched his language.

But what protection does the Fundamental Standard Interpretation offer someone who is accused of using a word that *sounds* like a term "commonly understood to convey direct and visceral hatred or contempt for human beings on the basis of their sex, race," etc.? It might be answered that it is, first of all, unlikely that such an accusation will be made. After all, what we do want to get at are the egregious cases of verbal harassment, and how else get at them except with a speech code? But what about a male's deliberately calling a female student a "witch" rather than a "bitch," or a white calling a black a "chigger" rather than a "nigger"? Does that get him off the hook? Or are these terms the "equivalent" of an epithet? (See the quotation from Grey below, at n. 53.)

I don't mean to be nitpicking here; no code is perfect, and all codes need to be interpreted. However, in order to determine whether some given term has been used as the equivalent of an epithet, we would have to look at the intention of the speaker. But it is precisely this kind of inquiry, once we go beyond a definite list of words, that leads to the fear that "however artfully drawn, [codes] can chill a good deal of provocative expression that is altogether desirable," and "that those who carry unpopular messages are being told to be quiet," as the Duke Rules put it.

Now, one does hope that the Stanford community is knowledgeable enough to make proper distinctions, that enforcement of the policy will be intelligent, and that problem cases, if they arise, will be handled sagaciously. But the opportunity for misunderstanding is present, unfortunately, even for a code that is as finely drawn as Stanford's, and how much more so for more loosely formulated codes! There is little protection afforded by any code against overzealous administrators.

Granted, the Interpretation does require that the speaker "*intended* to insult or stigmatize," in order to hold him or her guilty of harassment by vilification. In contrast to some other campus speech codes, strict liability is rejected. But intent is difficult to prove. More than likely, though, it is the accused who will be put in the difficult position of establishing that he had no such intent.[51] As a number of cases show, and as cases told to me by those involved indicate, a presumption of innocence does not always hold and the disciplinary procedures are not always fair.[52] And even if the accused is found innocent, or the charges are eventually dropped, he will have gone through a terrible ordeal. Recall, again, the case of Professor Gordon Snyder, whose lecture was misunderstood by a student. One has to hope that Thomas Grey will be sitting as a member of all discipline panels.

Now I don't mean to get into a "battle of the anecdotes" here: as against Jacobowitz and Howard one could juxtapose the Ujamaa incident. Slurs, epithets, and vulgarity—no matter to whom they may be directed, and whether or not face-to-face—should be condemned, and maintaining a positive message of civility is important. But more crucial than the outlawing of single words—which is *almost* acceptable to me—is the general effect on the expression of ideas.

What, then, about *ideas* that stigmatize a group? Ideas, too, can "convey direct and visceral hatred or contempt," for instance, the idea that blacks are intellectually inferior to others. Plainly, a statement to this effect, with or without a gutter epithet, can be as wounding as racial slurs alone. If one wants to penalize "wounding words" it makes no sense to single out gutter epithets, as the African American academic Henry Louis Gates says.

Professor Grey takes up this question. Imagine, he says, this scenario:

> [A] student's habit of loudly proclaiming his admiration for *The Bell Curve* around the dormitory becomes the target of protest by African-American students, who say it is aimed at (and certainly has the effect of) making them feel unwelcome in the university and making it more difficult to do their work. He refuses to stop, and the dispute gets into the campus newspaper, which quotes the offending student as saying that he has no intention of letting "a bunch of affirmative action morons" silence him, and that he hopes "what I'm saying will get some of them to think about whether they are really qualified to be here. . . ."
>
> Under the Stanford policy that was invalidated, the result would be clear: the white student could be freely criticized, but he would not be in violation of University disciplinary standards. No racial epithet or its equivalent has been addressed to a targeted individual.[53]

Grey's claim is reassuring for those who want controversial ideas to be protected, although his remarks make it plain that the Stanford policy doesn't get to the heart of forestalling "wounded identity." Why shouldn't the student's assertions, "wounding words," after all, be regarded as the equivalent of a racial epithet? True, there was no targeted individual in Grey's example, but we can imagine a case in which there is such a one. As for Professor Lawrence, I am not sure what his position is. Lawrence, as we saw before, is really concerned with more than "fighting words," that is, with the *content* of racist speech, the *message* of inferiority that it conveys. The Stanford code seems to be a fallback position for him.

I conclude, so far, that campus speech codes, even one as good as Stanford's, have serious formulation and enforcement problems, and it seems to me that *Chaplinsky* doesn't help Professor Lawrence's argument. I am not happy with this result, though. In any event, demeaning assertions should be combated by counterargument, not by punitive sanctions.

There is little doubt, on the other side, that racist speech may have a distorting effect on the operation of the marketplace of ideas. Lawrence argues this point in great detail, against civil libertarians who reject all speech restrictions on marketplace grounds.[54] He maintains that regulation of racist speech makes the intellectual climate more free, not less free: equality in the marketplace of ideas must be attained before speech can be truly free or debate can be fair. And he apparently therefore would hold that the traditional civil libertarian cure of "more speech" won't help, since the minority group is always bound to lose (but compare the Jehovah's Witnesses, who have generally won).[55] However, it is not only racist speech that distorts the market. And the attempt to police all speech that might adversely affect the marketplace of ideas would be infeasible and intolerable.

I further admit that the face-to-face use of fighting words and racial slurs, in particular, may have a "silencing" effect on their recipient that impedes free trade in ideas, which trade is the work of the university, because they can impede discussion. ("More speech" will not always immediately work against a targeted attack.) This is true generally of uncivil discourse. Of course, many academic exchanges are quite heated, and the line is sometimes crossed. Again, though, it is the role of teachers to educate students on what the boundaries are and to show them by example that civil debate promotes the search for truth. As for society at large, I don't see any way of raising the level of discourse at present; the crudity and vulgarity of politics and of the media and entertainment industries are too well entrenched. And universities are not far behind. Witness the courses whose aim seems to be to titillate.

NOTES

1. Samuel Walker, *Hate Speech: The History of an American Controversy* (Lincoln: University of Nebraska Press, 1994), 133. The essential factor in this success was that the movement had more or less organized advocates. On the other side, strong advocacy groups, e.g., the American Civil Liberties Union, are the reason why the United States has its extensive constitutional free speech protections, according to Walker.

2. *Doe v. Univ. of Michigan*, 721 F. Supp. 852 (E.D. Mich. 1989) (speech code effectively declared unconstitutional); *UMW Post v. Board of Regents of the Univ. of Wisconsin*, 774 F. Supp. 1163 (E.D. Wis. 1991) (speech code effectively declared unconstitutional); *R.A.V. v. City of St. Paul*, 505 U.S. 377 (1992) (hate crime ordinance declared unconstitutional). An abridgement of the opinion in *Doe v. Univ. of Michigan* is given in appendix A as an example of the courts' treatment of campus codes.

3. For a study of the cases, see Timothy C. Shiell, *Campus Hate Speech on Trial* (Lawrence: University of Kansas Press, 1998).

4. An even vaguer code was instituted at Central Michigan University after the *Doe* case in the same federal jurisdiction had declared such codes unconstitutional; it too was eventually found unconstitutional in *Dambrot v. Central Michigan University*, 55 F.3d 1177 (6th Cir. 1995).

5. This has been told me by a number of law professors, though law schools are just the place for taking up touchy issues. A notorious instance was the moot court competition at NYU Law School in 1990. The issue assigned for argument was whether a father could obtain custody of his child on the grounds that its mother was a lesbian. As is typical, some students were assigned to argue on one side and some on the other, but those assigned for the petitioner objected: the question, it was said, is not even debatable. The Moot Court Board decided that the issue was not "appropriate." In fact, it is the sort of issue that lawyers confront in the real world. For a description of the incident, see Nat Hentoff, *Free Speech for Me—But Not for Thee* (New York: HarperCollins, 1992), 202–16.

6. Documented in A. C. Kors and H. A. Silverglate, *The Shadow University: The Betrayal of Liberty on America's Campuses* (New York: Free Press, 1998), 176. The stifling of expression by "atmosphere" is well documented in Hentoff, *Free Speech*.

7. See *Healy v. James*, 408 U.S. 169 (1972) (upholding, on First Amendment grounds, the SDS's right to official recognition at Central Connecticut State College).

8. "Protest THIS!" is a university-funded student humor newspaper that offended racial and gender sensibilities. The issue had fake advertisements (for "MastaCard" and for the "Asian Student Alliance," with pictures of blacks and Asians). The paper's staff is racially and ethnically diverse, and the ads were done by minorities. An earlier issue ran a fictitious story saying rape counselors were tired of victims' "whining." University President Trachtenberg opposes continued funding of "Protest THIS!", but also said that it probably deserves "a chance to do better." *Washington Post*, May 17, 1998, B10.

9. It is also the case that administrations will defend rather questionable campus activities. The notorious 1997 SUNY/New Paltz Women's Studies conference, "Revolting Behavior: The Challenges of Women's Sexual Freedom," had a workshop on sadomasochism, which was recommended as an alternative way of loving. The president of the school defended it on grounds of academic freedom. But suppose a group of men had put on a pornography conference. I doubt very much that it would have received the same defense. Ironically, the New Paltz conference would have violated provisions of the Indianapolis antipornography ordinance inspired by the feminists Catharine MacKinnon and Andrea Dworkin. This ordinance banned sexually explicit works in which "women are presented as sexual objects who enjoy pain or humiliation." The ordinance was struck down in *American Booksellers Ass'n v. Hudnut*, 771 F.2d 323 (7th Cir. 1985). It has been reported to me that in some Duke women's studies courses men have been made the subject of ribald humor. I cannot vouch for the truth of the report, but I doubt that a course in which women were similarly treated would escape serious administrative objection.

10. The Supreme Court has gone beyond protection of merely offensive speech. In 1949 it upheld the right of a racist to give a speech that "vigorously, if not viciously" insulted various racial and political groups. *Terminiello v. Chicago*, 337 U.S. 1 (1949).

11. The code, instituted in 1981, restricts faculty speech as part of its rules banning harassment. It forbids faculty members from slurring students according to race, gender, ethnicity, etc., and also makes punishable the use of teaching techniques that make "the instructional setting hostile or intimidating, or demeaning" to students according to their group. Although no faculty member has been disciplined under the code, some have been subjected to long investigations for possible violations—which is enough to make others wary. In contrast to the student code, which was held unconstitutional in 1991 (see n. 2),

the faculty code has not been challenged in the courts. See "U. of Wisconsin Considers Proposal to Ease Limits on Faculty Speech," *Chronicle of Higher Education*, October 2, 1998, A14. On March 1, 1999, the faculty voted 71–62 to abolish the code provisions relating to instructional settings.

12. One is reminded here of the notorious incident of the torture and murder of Emmett Till, a fourteen-year-old black youth, in Mississippi in 1955. While the facts of the case are somewhat confused and obscure, Till apparently made a pass, including a leer or "wolf whistle," at a white woman, and thereby violated the sexual line between black males and white women. See Stephen J. Whitfield, *A Death in the Delta* (New York: Free Press, 1988). This incident had a galvanizing effect on the black civil rights movement.

13. See, generally, David A. Hoekema, *Campus Rules and Moral Community: In Place of* In Loco Parentis (Lanham, Md.: Rowman & Littlefield, 1994). The trend continues; see "In a Revolution of Rules, Campuses Go Full Circle," *New York Times*, March 3, 1999, A1.

14. M. J. Matsuda, C. R. Lawrence III, R. Delgado, and K. W. Crenshaw, *Words That Wound: Critical Race Theory, Assaultive Speech and the First Amendment* (Boulder, Colo.: Westview Press, 1993). With slight editorial changes and the elimination of some footnotes, this book reprints previously published articles by the first three authors. The introduction describes the origins and aims of Critical Race Theory. Quotations are from this book.

15. 87 *Michigan Law Rev.* (1989), 2320–81. This article is reprinted in *Words That Wound,* 17–52.

16. See Walker, *Hate Speech*, 46ff. Though there are earlier group libel laws, the only hate speech law enacted in the 1930s was a 1934 New Jersey law, enacted as a result of clashes between Nazi and anti-Nazi groups. The law prohibited "propaganda or statements creating or tending to create prejudice, hostility, hatred, ridicule, disgrace or contempt of people . . . by reason of their race, color, creed or manner of worship." It was used to prosecute a Jehovah's Witness who distributed anti-Catholic literature. In an opinion that invoked Holmes's "marketplace of ideas," the law was overturned on constitutional free speech grounds (*State v. Klapprott*, 22 A. 2d 877 (1941)). A number of speech cases have involved members of the Jehovah's Witnesses, on which see Walker's book.

17. David Riesman, "Democracy and Defamation," 42 *Columbia Law Review* (1942), 729–80, 1085–1123, 1282–1318. Noting the danger to freedom of speech, Riesman later reversed himself.

18. Regarding campus speech, see Richard Delgado, "Campus Anti-racism Rules: Constitutional Narratives in Collision," 85 *Northwestern Univ. Law Rev.* (1991), 343–87. This article describes a clash between a First Amendment narrative, marketplace interpretations of law and politics, and an equal protection one. Racial slurs, says Delgado, "contribute little to the discovery of truth" (379). I don't think that this article adds anything fundamentally new to the article cited in the next footnote, which is discussed in the text. Professor Delgado helped draft the University of Wisconsin policy, invalidated in *UMW Post*, cited in n. 2.

19. See Richard Delgado, "Words That Wound: A Tort Action for Racial Insults, Epithets, and Name-Calling," 17 *Harvard Civil Rights-Civil Liberties Law Rev.* (1982), 138–81. This article is reprinted in *Words That Wound*, 89–110.

20. *Words That Wound*, 100.

21. *Words That Wound*, 107.

22. The leading proponent of the high-value/low-value distinction is Cass R. Sunstein. See Sunstein, "Pornography and the First Amendment," *Duke Law J.* (1986), 589–627, especially 602–08. Among the factors relevant to determining low-value speech are its distance from the "central concern" of the First Amendment and its noncognitive appeal. Sunstein is criticized in Larry Alexander, "Low Value Speech," 83 *Northwestern Univ. Law*

Rev. (1989), 547–54. See also Kent Greenawalt, *Fighting Words* (Princeton, N.J.: Princeton University Press, 1995), 87f., 102ff.

23. The elements of the cause of action for racial insult are not formulated with reference to a particular race: "In order to prevail in an action for a racial insult, the plaintiff should be required to prove that language was addressed to him or her by the defendant that was intended to demean through reference to race; that the plaintiff understood and intended to demean through reference to race; and that a reasonable person would recognize as a racial insult." *Words That Wound*, 109. The word "demean," which occurs in many campus speech codes too, is not defined. But the last provision may take care of the problem. Still, how is the speaker to know whether something will be taken as demeaning?

24. Presumably, there must be a definite audience; "Niggers be damned" would not be enough to satisfy the criteria for a cause of action or a campus violation unless said in the presence of a black or, if put on a poster, it is seen by a black. It is sometimes said that some people can't be insulted, apparently because they have such a low opinion of themselves that they do not perceive the remark as denigrating, or because they *are* contemptible. It seems to be Delgado's position that a racial slur makes black recipients *feel* bad, as objects of contempt.

25. See n. 16.

26. There are continuous calls to punish anti-Semitic and antiblack vandalism as hate crimes, but the *R.A.V.* case (n. 2) undercuts the effort. On the legal wrangling over the Skokie march, see Walker, *Hate Speech*, 120–25. The National Socialist Party eventually won its case but didn't hold the march; it did get what it wanted: publicity.

27. The term "anti-Semitism" was invented by Wilhelm Marr (1818–1902), the founder of the German League of Anti-Semites in 1879. Marr's opposition to Jews was not on religious grounds, but rather that they were an "alien" race, a charge that goes back to the ancient world. In current American white-supremacist literature, Jews are said to be not a religious group, but an Asiatic race, "locked in mortal combat with Aryan man." See Adolph Hitler, *Mein Kampf*, trans. Ralph Mannheim (Boston: Houghton Mifflin, 1943), Vol. I, Chapter 11. On December 9, 1998, the fiftieth anniversary of the convention against genocide, the UN General Assembly decided to list anti-Semitism as a form of racism.

28. Politicization is "the practice of misstating or distorting or denying a truth or judgment for which adequate grounds can be given, in behalf of a partisan political cause, whether it be a revolutionary or a counterrevolutionary one." Politicization is different from partisanship, taking sides on a controversial issue.

29. A number of anti-Semitic Web sites purporting to be based on "scholarship" are devoted to Holocaust denial. This is not to say that there aren't open issues about its interpretation, its causes, etc. See www.hatewatch.org, which also has links to all sorts of hate organizations (antiblack, anti-Catholic, anti-Muslim, etc.). White-supremacist groups tend to be anti-Semitic as well as antiblack.

30. "To what an extent the whole existence of this people is based on a continuous lie is shown incomparably by the *Protocols of the Wise Men of Zion*, so infinitely hated by the Jews." Hitler, *Mein Kampf*, 307. This work is an anti-Semitic forgery aimed at showing the existence of an international Jewish conspiracy bent on world domination. Its latest version was concocted in Paris at the end of the nineteenth century by an unknown author working for the Russian secret police. Translated into many languages, the work received wide circulation, and was sponsored in the United States by Henry Ford until 1927. Nazi propaganda heavily relied on it and it has been reissued in Arab states.

31. Henry Louis Gates, Jr., "Let Them Talk," *New Republic*, September 20, 27, 1993, 37–49, at 45. This article is a review of *Words That Wound*.

32. *Duke Law Journal* (1990), 431–83. Reprinted in *Words That Wound*, 53–88.

33. *Beauharnais v. Illinois*, 343 U.S. 250 (1952). The Illinois law prohibited publication of material that portrayed the "depravity, criminality, unchastity, or lack of virtue of a class of citizens, of any race, color, creed or religion." The law was passed as a result of a race riot in East St. Louis in 1917. Most commentators doubt that *Beauharnais* is still "good law"; a group libel law would not be upheld today. For a discussion see Walker, chapter 5.

34. "I do not contend that *all* conduct with an expressive component should be treated as unprotected speech. To the contrary, my suggestion that *racist* conduct amounts to speech is premised on a unique characteristic of racism—namely its reliance upon the defamatory message of white supremacy to achieve its injurious purpose" (*Words That Wound*, 60). "Racism is both 100 percent speech and 100 percent conduct" (62).

35. *Words That Wound*, 75. See appendix B, regarding "subordination."

36. See Catharine A. MacKinnon, *Only Words* (Cambridge, Mass.: Harvard University Press, 1993). We shall not deal with the feminist argument here. It is my view that problems similar to those found in the critical race theorists' position obtain also for MacKinnon's approach.

37. This issue was presented some years ago in the classic article by Herbert Wechsler, "Toward Neutral Principles of Constitutional Law," 73 *Harvard Law Review*, 1–35 (1959). "Is the state forbidden to effectuate a will that draws a racial line, a will that can accomplish any disposition only through the aid of law, or is it a sufficient answer that the discrimination was the testator's and not the state's? May not the state employ its law to vindicate the privacy of property against a trespasser, regardless of the grounds of his exclusion, or does it embrace the owner's reasons for excluding if it buttresses his power by the law" (29–30). It is precisely Wechsler's search for "neutral principles" that the critical race theorists reject.

38. *Words That Wound*, 63 (emphasis in original).

39. Gates, "Let Them Talk," 48.

40. Though I think he exaggerates, there is truth to what Jonathan Rauch says: "We would all like to think that knowledge could be separated from hurt. We would all like to think that painful but useful 'legitimate' criticism is objectively distinguishable from criticism which is merely ugly and hurtful. . . . [In] the pursuit of knowledge many people . . . will be hurt, and that this is a reality which no amount of wishing or regulating can ever change." *Kindly Inquisitors* (Chicago: University of Chicago Press, 1993), 125, 126. Academic reviews sometimes involve a direct assault on an author's character, reputation, or competence, and can be quite wounding to one's psyche and career.

41. In February 1995 a judge of the Santa Clara County (California) Superior Court struck down the Stanford University speech code on the basis of California's 1992 Leonard Law: Private educational institutions (excepting religious institutions) may not discipline a student "solely on the basis of . . . speech or other communication that when engaged in outside the campus is protected from government restriction by the First Amendment." The university chose not to appeal this decision. The story of the Stanford code, with a vigorous defense of its legality, is told by its main drafter. See Thomas C. Grey, "How to Write a Speech Code Without Really Trying: Reflections on the Stanford Experience," 29 *U.C. Davis L. Rev.* 891–956 (1996). Professor Grey says that the Stanford policy was mislabeled as a speech code by the court. The policy, Grey maintains, sought to protect expression by narrowly defining the area of prohibited speech.

42. *Words That Wound*, 66. Although *Chaplinsky* has not been explicitly overruled, its validity has been eroded by some later decisions, including *Cohen*. See Gerald Gunther, *Constitutional Law*, 12th ed. (Westbury, N.Y.: Foundation Press, 1991), 1073–75.

43. *Chaplinsky v. New Hampshire*, 315 U.S. 568 (1942), 572 (emphasis added), 573. Any governmental regulation of speech, aside from the "certain well-defined and narrowly limited classes" (and Murphy's list does not purport to be exhaustive), must be content- and viewpoint-neutral, in the terminology of later First Amendment doctrine.

44. The Fundamental Standard Interpretation is given in Grey, 947–48; *Words That Wound*, 67. The Fundamental Standard, as written in 1996, reads: "Students at Stanford are expected to show both within and without the University such respect for order, morality, personal honor and the rights of others as is demanded of good citizens. Failure to do this will be sufficient cause for removal from the University."

45. Grey, 905–6 (emphasis added).

46. In its effort to prevent wounded identity, the Stanford code is much more restrained than Michigan's, whose Interpretive Guide penalized such actions as failing to invite a student of another race, sex, etc., to a floor party or study group, laughing at an improper joke, or commenting in a derogatory way on the physical appearance of another person or group. See *Doe v. Univ. of Michigan*, n. 2, at 857. Professor Lawrence thinks that Michigan's code was "sloppy." "It is almost as if the university administrators purposely wrote an unconstitutional regulation so that they could say to the Black students, 'We tried to help you, but the courts just won't let us do it.'" *Words That Wound*, 84.

47. Duke University Law School's "Rules, Policies, and Procedures," www.law.duke.edu/general/info/s11.html#policy11-5 (Dean's Statement on Freedom of Expression in the Law School).

48. See the quotation from Grey, at n. 53 ("a racial epithet or its *equivalent*"). The water buffalo incident is described in detail in Kors and Silverglate, 9–33. The Penn code is quoted at page 11. The charges generated a body of scholarship on whether "water buffalo" is a racial epithet.

49. See, e.g., the case of Cornell Professor James Maas at the Web site of the Center for Individual Rights, www.wdn.com/cir/maas.htm. Cornell maintained a secret file on his alleged harassment, to which Maas was not given access. See, also, a lengthy account in Craig L. Hymowitz, "The Locked Box," *Heterodoxy* (May 1995), beginning on page 1. Of course, I am in no position to vouch for the complete accuracy of these accounts.

50. See *New York Times*, January 29, 1999, A8 ("Race Mix-Up Raises Havoc for Capital"). A similar incident is reported from Chicago. While presenting a bill to a Jewish patient, a dentist said, "Don't be afraid of chewing down on it." At his two-day hearing before the city human rights committee, the dentist kept lamely trying to argue that he was talking about the patient's new filling, not about a bargaining trait often attributed to Jews by their detractors. *Herald Sun* (Durham, N.C.), February 3, 1999, A10.

51. "Stigmatize" is a vague term and I am not clear on its scope. Someone who uses a "fighting word," as understood in the Interpretation, is likely to have the burden of showing lack of intent to stigmatize.

52. See Kors and Silverglate, and Hentoff, passim.

53. Grey, 924. Professor Grey is at this point arguing that the Stanford code is more protective of free speech than an alternative harassment code that very likely would have been upheld, but which would have had the flaw of the potentially chilling vagueness of hostile-environment discrimination (see chapter 5). Richard J. Herrnstein and Charles Murray, *The Bell Curve: Intelligence and Class in American Life* (New York: Free Press, 1994) is the subject of much debate.

54. *Words That Wound*, 76–87.

55. See n. 16.

Chapter Five

Campus Speech Restrictions II

If Professors Delgado and Lawrence are ambivalent on how far protection is extended to the expression of racist ideas, Mari J. Matsuda, also a critical race theorist, is clearer on the issue. Her primary concern is not racial slurs and epithets. She explicitly argues for restriction of racist hate "propaganda," and not only against blacks but also against Jews and others.[1] She too begins with the devastating effects of hate speech on its victims. But while Delgado proposes the remedy of a private civil tort action, Professor Matsuda suggests that "formal criminal and administrative sanction—public as opposed to private prosecution—is also an appropriate response to racist speech."[2] Like Delgado and Lawrence, she maintains that her proposal is consistent with the First Amendment; it is necessary to contextualize it and escape the "neutrality trap" of conventional civil liberties jurisprudence.

A novelty of Matsuda's argument is her use of international human rights law and the practices of other free and democratic countries. There are a number of treaties and declarations that call for government efforts to eliminate racist propaganda and to make certain forms of racist speech subject to criminal punishment. No doubt, the extermination of Jews and other groups during the Second World War was a factor. And as Matsuda notes, "the knowledge that anti-Semitic hate propaganda and the rise of Nazism were clearly connected guided development of the emerging international law on incitement to racial hatred."[3] Such countries as the United Kingdom, New Zealand, and Canada (see below) have enacted laws that criminalize some forms of racist speech. These laws may or may not be effective deterrents; in some cases they have been used to bring prosecutions against minority group members. The United States has been hesitant to adopt similar laws; the First Amendment has been seen as an obstacle. In this country, white-supremacist groups are free to spew their vicious doctrines.

THE VICTIM'S PERSPECTIVE AND HATE SPEECH

Professor Matsuda presents in detail what she maintains is "the structural reality of racism in the United States,"[4] which undergirds the claim that a legal response to it is required. Racism, which is endemic to our society and its institutions, is a form of, and an instrument of, *domination* over subordinate groups, a fact that is overlooked by conventional civil liberties jurisprudence. Racist speech and propaganda do not cause only psychic injury. When seen from the victim's perspective, they are in effect used to legitimate violence, as well as overt and covert disparate treatment. Racist speech, therefore, "is best treated as a sui generis category, presenting an idea so historically untenable, so dangerous, and so tied to the perpetuation of violence and degradation of the very classes of human beings who are least equipped to respond that it is properly treated as outside the realm of protected discourse."[5]

In contextualizing the First Amendment from the victim's perspective, Matsuda endorses a "non-neutral, value-laden" approach that would capture the worst forms of hate speech. In order to prevent opening the dreaded floodgates of censorship, she lays down three conditions that would have to be satisfied jointly as a prerequisite to prosecution:

1. The message is of racial inferiority;
2. The message is directed against a historically oppressed group;
3. The message is persecutory, hateful, and degrading.[6]

These elements narrow the field of interference with speech. Proclaiming the superiority of one race over another is permitted as long as the message isn't hateful and persecutory; satire and stereotyping are permitted as long as they aren't persecutory, as offensive as they might be.

And, it also follows: "Hateful verbal attacks upon dominant-group members by victims is [*sic*] permissible."[7] To me, this is an unwelcome conclusion. For though one can sympathize with the anger of a subjugated group, one also recalls that Matsuda emphasizes the causal connection between hateful words and violent action. Matsuda, it appears, endorses a kind of double standard and viewpoint discrimination: much depends on who uses hate speech. She does admit that there are problem cases, as when a member of a subordinated group speaks hatefully of a member of another subordinated group. Zionism presents such a problem case for her.

"I reject," says Professor Matsuda, "the sweeping charge that Zionism is racism and argue instead for a highly contextualized consideration of Zionist speech." Therefore, a Zionist's racist speech that is a reaction to historical persecution is protected. But if the speaker is white and chooses to ally with a historically dominant group, the speaker loses the privilege. "Again," she says, "it is important to add that the various subordinated communities are best equipped to analyze and condemn hate speech arising within their midst."[8]

Matsuda, then, accepts the idea of "victim's privilege": only the victim or subordinated community can determine what is offensive, and she thereby opens up a can of worms. Suppose Zionists are alleged to have spoken hatefully about Arabs and Arabs' policies toward Israel, and Arabs respond in kind. Were the speeches by either side racist? Which side is a historically subordinated group, or a "more" subordinated group? It seems clear that any trial of these issues would turn into a rancorous political dispute. A court will be faced with political arguments and partisan versions of history. While it must be conceded that Professor Matsuda considers such cases (and other instances can be imagined) to be "hard," the looseness of her position emerges on the question whether blacks and other minorities may engage in hateful anti-Semitic speech. All she says is, "I am inclined to prohibit such speech."[9] Matsuda claims to be putting forward "narrow" grounds for interfering with free speech and for getting at the worst offenders. Should the scope of freedom of speech then turn on Professor Matsuda's inclination?

I find it interesting that Matsuda is also "inclined" to criminalize the "cold-blooded" version of anti-Semitism, such as Holocaust denial, that is "cunningly devoid of explicit hate language."[10] Here, the difficulty of securing a conviction would be in establishing that "the message is persecutory, hateful, and degrading." On the other hand, Matsuda is prepared to countenance an academic forum for the "dead-wrong social scientist" who puts forth a thesis of racial inferiority, as long as it is supported by evidence acceptable in the relevant discipline. Such theses, she says, should be dealt with in open debate. I agree with the last assertion, but I do think that some dissonance is to be detected in her position. Perhaps, though, the matter should not be pressed, for Professor Matsuda regards the second case as a "difficult" one. In any event, these examples bring us back to the topic of campus speech.

THE UNIVERSITY AS SAFE HARBOR

We have seen that Matsuda is prepared to subject to legal sanctions speech that satisfies certain "narrow" conditions. The case of the university, she however says, "raises unique concerns."[11] She describes in some detail how college students are at a vulnerable stage of psychological development. Students, she says, "are particularly dependent on the university, for intellectual development, and for self-definition. Official tolerance of racist speech in this setting is more harmful than generalized tolerance in the community at large."[12]

Unfortunately, in this article, Professor Matsuda does not spell out exactly what she would propose for the campus. I think, though, it is fair to assume that she would endorse a speech code, at least like Stanford's if not something more drastic, for reasons explored earlier regarding Delgado and Lawrence. Moreover, since she is anxious to prohibit racial "propaganda," and not just epithets and fighting words, she would extend her three criteria of criminalizable speech to the university, though in what way is not entirely clear to me. The problematic cases are sanitized racism and "cold-blooded" anti-Semitism. Should these be prohibited, given the "vulnerability" of university students? Racial propaganda—

hateful messages that aim at conversion—not only causes distress to victims, but it also instills or reinforces pernicious prejudices in others. The question is complicated because we might want to distinguish between in-class and out-of-class statements and between faculty and students.

In order to better understand Matsuda's "argument from vulnerability," and to be in a position to evaluate it, it is useful to look at the 1990 Canadian case, *R. v. Keegstra*.[13] This case is apposite, in part, because the majority of the Supreme Court of Canada adopts a position very much like the one Matsuda would have us adopt regarding the First Amendment. Keegstra was convicted under a law "which prohibits the wilful promotion of hatred, other than in private conversation, towards any section of the public distinguished by colour, race, religion or ethnic origin." Keegstra averred that this law violates the guarantee of freedom of expression found in the *Canadian Charter of Rights and Freedoms*, and appealed his conviction.Without delving into the complex procedural issues, we present the facts of the case as stated by the court:

> Mr. James Keegstra was a high school teacher in Eckville, Alberta from the early 1970s until his dismissal in 1982. In 1984 Mr. Keegstra was charged under . . . the *Criminal Code* with unlawfully promoting hatred against an identifiable group by communicating anti-semitic statements to his students.
>
> Mr. Keegstra's teachings attributed various evil qualities to Jews. He thus described Jews to his pupils as "treacherous," "subversive," "sadistic," "money-loving," "power hungry" and "child killers." He taught his classes that Jewish people seek to destroy Christianity and are responsible for depressions, anarchy, chaos, wars and revolution. According to Mr. Keegstra, Jews "created the Holocaust to gain sympathy" and, in contrast to open and honest Christians, were said to be deceptive, secretive and inherently evil. Mr. Keegstra expected his students to reproduce his teachings in class and on exams. If they failed to do so, their marks suffered.

Apparently, most of Keegstra's class time was taken up with these matters; it was always easy for his students to divert him to them.

By a 4–3 majority, the court upheld the conviction. The rationale of the majority was much in line with that underlying the international law and human rights documents referred to by Professor Matsuda, as well as considerations germane to the Canadian situation—a good example of freedom of expression contextualized, as it were. The sharply worded dissent heavily relied on the marketplace-of-ideas concept of conventional First Amendment jurisprudence.[14]

James Keegstra, it is quite clear, was not just spouting "cold-blooded" or sanitized anti-Semitism; his was anti-Semitism of the most open and virulent sort, which he expected his students to absorb. Second, while the court mentions that his was a high school class (which included ninth-graders), this fact plays no explicit role in the opinions. Plainly, though, Keegstra was propagandizing and trying to convert to his view a captive audience of defenseless, vulnerable youths. This was politicization at its worst.

Now, how would Keegstra fare in a U.S. court, and how would Professor Matsuda approach the issue? It is pretty clear that the criminal law under which Keegstra was convicted would not survive constitutional muster,[15] while Matsuda would defend it. More interesting, and a bit more speculative, is the question of whether Keegstra's dismissal would survive. The Supreme Court has recognized the general power of school boards and principals to control the content of curriculums, and to determine what is educationally suitable. Questions have arisen over the power of school boards to remove from a high school library books that they regard as vulgar, too focused on sex, and racist. In a 5–4 plurality judgment, i.e., there was no single opinion to which a majority agreed, in *Board of Education v. Pico* the Court held that the board did not have such power.[16] Writing for three other members, Justice William Brennan emphasized the limited nature of the question being decided: the removal of books originally placed in a library by school authorities.

On the other hand, the Supreme Court has recognized a limited right of academic freedom for public school teachers, but it does not accord them a free hand to do whatever they wish in their courses. The Court does seem to accept that public school students are "vulnerable" in the way that Matsuda describes. There probably are a variety of grounds on which a Keegstra could be dismissed, particularly his commandeering of a classroom to preach a highly partisan political view. It is highly doubtful that a teacher's right goes so far as to allow the Keegstras of this world to propagate their hate messages in a public elementary or high school. In his concurring opinion in *Pico*, Justice Harry Blackmun suggests that "school officials may seek to instill certain values 'by persuasion and example,' . . . or by choice of emphasis."[17] The values he mentions are the guarantees of civil liberty, patriotism, and love of country. One may also suppose that they include the values of equality and human dignity, as well as hard work and honesty.

Most interesting for us is Justice Rehnquist's dissent. He distinguishes between elementary and high schools, on the one side, and universities, on the other. School libraries, unlike university libraries, are not designed for freewheeling inquiry. More generally, writes Rehnquist:

> When [the government] acts as an educator, at least at the elementary and secondary school level, the government is engaged in inculcating values and knowledge in relatively impressionable young people.
>
> Education consists in the selective presentation of ideas. The effective acquisition of knowledge depends upon an orderly exposure to relevant information. Nowhere is this more true than in elementary and secondary schools, where, unlike the broad-ranging inquiry available to university students, the courses taught are those thought most relevant to the young students' individual development. Of necessity, elementary and secondary educators must separate the relevant from the irrelevant, the appropriate from the inappropriate.[18]

Unfortunately, Justice Rehnquist does not spell out what the appropriate and inappropriate are. But what is important here is the distinction drawn between universities and elementary and high schools, a distinction reinforced by later decisions. I think that U.S. courts would be very much inclined to uphold the dismissal of John Keegstra and his ilk from elementary or high school teaching.

Universities are places for freewheeling inquiry, though, and allow for much more latitude in an instructor's speech. There are a number of cases going back at least to the 1957 case of *Sweezy v. New Hampshire*, which are concerned with the "chilling effect" that regulation of speech may have in universities.[19] The special status of universities is expressed in passing by Chief Justice Rehnquist in *Rust v. Sullivan*: "[We] have recognized that the university is a traditional sphere of free expression so fundamental to the functioning of our society that the Government's ability to control speech within that sphere by means of conditions attached to the expenditure of Government funds is restricted by the vagueness and overbreadth doctrines of the First Amendment."[20]

The special status of universities as places of freewheeling and broad-ranging inquiry has implications for the scope of free speech. These implications are recognized both by the U.S. Supreme Court and by the university's own constitution. The question before us, then, is whether college and university students are so vulnerable, as Matsuda claims, that "official tolerance of racist speech in this setting is more harmful than generalized tolerance in the community at large." This question is in part an empirical one and cannot be discussed fully here.

The view that students are vulnerable has lead to a revival of the in loco parentis doctrine. We now find a greater interest in the mentoring of students, a concern about drinking and community building, and so on. A recent newspaper report describes ". . . two questions that are emerging as central: Are undergraduates really adults? And should they be seen as the college's customers or more as its products?"[21] Now, I am prepared to agree that college and university undergraduates are vulnerable individuals in some respects. The issue for us is how far this consideration should affect the regulation of campus speech.

No doubt, for many students the university is *intellectually* a dangerous place. Because it is a place of freewheeling, searching, and in-depth inquiries, it is a place where their beliefs and prejudices may well be shaken; courses in history, science, and philosophy, among other courses, are notorious for their effect on students' beliefs. Students take a risk when they enter a college or university. And universities acquire a correlative responsibility: that the faculty be academically competent and committed to the pursuit of truth. To be sure, many students are socially and intellectually immature, a fact that imposes various pedagogical obligations on faculty. But one thing that the university cannot do is guarantee students a "safe harbor" when it comes to the expression of ideas. Perhaps here, though, we should distinguish between in-class and out-of-class statements and between faculty and students.

According to Rodney A. Smolla, a professor of constitutional law, a professor is an intellectual free agent but not a behavioral free agent. The university, he suggests, should be allowed, and maybe has an obligation, to police speech attacks by faculty in classrooms. Since the teacher is an officer of the university, especially in a public institution there is a governmental interest in controlling the content of its own speech and ensuring that it is not racially or sexually abusive.[22]

The on-campus, out-of-class statements of faculty and students presumably are under academic freedom and First Amendment privileges.[23]

Although partisanship and controversial opinions have a legitimate place in the classroom, it would seem, on this view, that a professor could—and even should—be "disciplined" for in-class statements that are blatant expressions of racial or sexual contempt; for instance, statements using the sort of language James Keegstra did about Jews. Clearly, at least some of such language conveys "direct and visceral hatred or contempt," in the words of the Stanford code. I assume that such expressions of contempt are "abusive," but perhaps are so only if directed toward a particular student, or if there are blacks or women in the class. Possibly, the professor could be fired, though there may be problems, if he or she is tenured.

I presume though that blatant in-class expressions of contempt or abuse are very rare these days and that a professor who is in this frame of mind will be more guarded in his or her speech. The difficult problems arise when the statements are occasional or incidental, rather than a constant barrage like Keegstra's; or, more difficult, when some students *take* some statement to be contemptuous or abusive.[24] Suppose, for instance, a male professor says that a woman's place is in the home rather than in a career; or a female professor says that all acts of intercourse are acts of rape, implying that men are rapists. Are either of these contemptuous or abusive? Maybe, but maybe not. Statements that are less than Keegstra's vitriol raise again some of the problems we have found in speech codes.

What about the in-class, blatant statements of racial contempt made by students? Here, I think, the best approach is criticism, by the professor and other students. This does not mean that a racist student necessarily will be argued out of his position and come to a change of mind. But other vulnerable students are far less likely to be taken in by him.

But there is another aspect to this sort of case, which I surmise is also very rare. Such statements are likely to be highly disruptive to the orderly conduct of a course, and therefore are subject to control by the instructor. Imagine a student who shouts out "BULLSHIT!" in class. Surely, the instructor may chastise him or even "kick him out" if the practice continues. So also, if vitriolic racial statements have a disruptive effect, the same procedure could be adopted. Kicking someone out, though, may be more easily said than done. The real problem, these days, is real disruptions by students who don't like what the instructor has said or the language he used—"Indian" for "Native American," for instance. University administrations have shown a remarkable lack of backbone in dealing with such disruptions.

Critical examination of blatant statements of racial contempt, however, is still the best approach, lest the student become resentful and more confirmed in his racism. I think that this latter outcome may well be the effect of speech codes that prohibit expression and thus silence students who hold such views. Moreover, one can't begin to conduct a discussion if the view you would criticize is outlawed or prevented from being heard. Of course, it requires a lot of self-restraint to have a discussion with a blatant racist. In fact, blatant contempt, whether it comes from faculty or students, is likely to arouse an extreme, negative reaction from the audience.

SANITIZED RACISM AND ANTI-SEMITISM

Let us turn to the more important question of *in-class* expressions of "cold-blooded" racism and anti-Semitism, racism and anti-Semitism that are "cunningly devoid of explicit hate language," as Professor Matsuda says. The distinction between this type and the blatant variety is primarily one of content or form of expression. Cases in point are some, perhaps all, instances of Holocaust denial and allegations of the relative mental inferiority of blacks. As we have seen, Matsuda is inclined to criminalize the cold-blooded version of anti-Semitism, while she is prepared to countenance an academic forum for the "dead-wrong social scientist" who puts forth a thesis of racial inferiority, as long as it is supported by evidence acceptable in the relevant discipline. It is supported, I suppose, by the *type* of evidence generally used, though the specific evidence is widely rejected in the discipline. As mentioned earlier, the difficulty of securing a criminal conviction would be in establishing that "the message is persecutory, hateful, and degrading."

Because of the vulnerability of university students, as Matsuda says, "official tolerance of racist speech in this setting is more harmful than generalized tolerance in the community at large," and it would seem that they might need protection from cold-blooded as well as blatant racism. But the two sorts may not always be easy to distinguish. The cold-blooded variety is in fact more subtle and insidious than the latter, and students might be more easily taken in by it. Cold-blooded racism and anti-Semitism cunningly present themselves as the "truth," based on scholarly research. The direct attack of critical evaluation is of course essential in such cases. For example, the Duke University history department did precisely the right thing when it responded to a Holocaust-denial advertisement in the student newspaper with a critical advertisement of its own.

Let us try to apply these considerations to a few aspects of the case of Anthony Martin, a longtime tenured professor of Africana Studies at Wellesley College, which is reported in the *Boston Globe*.[25] Our interest is in the issues of principle that it raises; the case is used here for purposes of illustration.

In the academic year of 1993–94, Professor Martin assigned a notoriously anti-Semitic book, *The Secret Relationship between Blacks and Jews* (1991), as required reading for his courses.[26] In language reminiscent of Henry Ford's world Jewish conspiracy theory, this book alleges that Jews dominated the African slave trade and bear a monumental responsibility for its evils: "Jews have been conclusively linked to the greatest endeavor ever undertaken against an entire race of people—the Black African Holocaust."[27]

Professor Martin was a controversial figure. His antipathy toward Jews was well known on the Wellesley campus, and in the mid-1980s he had been denied a merit raise, presumably because of dissatisfaction with his teaching on that account, though he had received such increases before. Martin sued and the case was settled out of court. His subsequent assignment of *The Secret Relationship* caused an uproar.[28] True, there were Jews in the slave trade but their role was rather marginal. Moreover, scholars in the field regard the book to be full of misquotations, distortions, and exaggerations, a book without credibility.[29] Martin is not just Professor Matsuda's "dead-wrong social scientist."

Now, what is wrong with assigning such a book? Would it be wrong to assign Hitler's *Mein Kampf* in a course on modern German history?[30] Certainly, it would not, despite Hitler's racist fulmination; it is an important document and worth study as such. But the case of *The Secret Relationship* is different: here we have typical anti-Semitic propaganda, not something presented as a pathological case worth studying; here we have falsehoods presented as true. (The book may of course contain some truths.) And as the *Boston Globe* quotes Wellesley professor Mary Lefkowitz, academic freedom does not grant a right to teach falsehoods in the classroom. Of course, instructors do assign books that contain falsehoods. But then the instructor has an obligation to point out those statements he or she believes to be false.

The Secret Relationship is sanitized anti-Semitism, "cunningly devoid of explicit hate language," but fundamentally false; in fact, it arguably consists of dangerous falsehoods.[31] The book does however contain *ideas*, ideas that Anthony Martin believes to be true and expects students to adopt. How to deal with someone, particularly a tenured faculty member, who teaches falsehoods but believes them to be true? Should a university's commitment to academic freedom, free speech, and First Amendment values protect such a person from dismissal from teaching? Or may such a person be dismissed for *academic misconduct*? What is to be done in a case such as this?

Remarks relevant to this issue are found in a recent federal court decision, *Feldman v. Ho*, in which there are a number of references to the notion of academic misconduct. It is speech, says Judge Easterbrook, "that lies at the core of scholarship, and every academic decision is in the end a decision about speech."[32] The judge then goes on to quote from an earlier decision of his:

> Teachers . . . speak and write for a living and are eager to protect both public and private interests in freedom to stake out controversial positions. Yet they also evaluate speech for a living and are eager to protect both public and private interests in the ability to judge the speech of others and to react adversely to some. They grade their students' papers and performance in class. They edit journals, which reject scholarly papers of poor quality. They evaluate their colleagues' academic writing and they deny continuing employment to professors whose speech does not meet their institutions standards of quality. . . . "The government" as an abstraction could not penalize any citizen for misunderstanding the views of Karl Marx or misrepresenting the political philosophy of James Madison, but a Department of Political Science can and should show such a person the door—and a public university may sack a professor of chemistry who insists on instructing his students in moral philosophy or publishes only romance novels. Every university evaluates and acts on the basis of speech by members of the faculty. . . .[33]

The commitment to freedom of speech, then, has a very *special* character in the university. It protects the expression of controversial opinions but it does not necessarily protect incompetence nor does it protect academic misconduct. The 1915 General Report of the Committee on Academic Freedom and Tenure of the American Association of University Professors declined to enumerate the grounds for dismissal of faculty members, but it did insist that if charged with "professional incompetency" the individual should have a fair trial on the issue.[34] While tenure has a sacred status in universities, especially for those faculty members who have it, there are conditions under which it can be lost. As Duke law professor William Van Alstyne says in an article defending the institution of tenure: "Tenure, accurately and unequivocally defined, lays no claim whatever to a guarantee of lifetime employment. Rather, tenure provides only that no person continuously retained as a full-time faculty member beyond a specified lengthy period of probationary service may thereafter be dismissed *without adequate cause*."[35]

What constitutes adequate cause? Unless an institution specifies its particulars, cases will be governed by the "common law" of academic professionalism. Plagiarism or the falsification of evidence in a scientific article would certainly seem to qualify as professional or academic misconduct. And so would the propagation of falsehoods as truths. I agree with Professor Lefkowitz that academic freedom does not grant a right to teach falsehoods in the classroom. A person who does so teach, in the words of Judge Easterbrook, can and should be shown the door.

It is, however, extremely difficult to dismiss a tenured professor on this ground. Universities do make judgments of academic quality in deciding whether to grant tenure, and the process can be rather complex. Since tenure is almost tantamount to a guarantee of lifetime employment, there usually has to be a demonstration of a higher standard of expertise and accomplishment than at the individual's initial hiring. *De*tenuring is even a more difficult affair; there will have to be a showing of professional incompetency or misconduct. In such a case, "due process" will have to be maintained, and the process will be long and involve the collection of evidence and counterevidence and a series of hearings before faculty and administrative boards. Unsurprisingly, such cases are likely to end up in the public courts.

These days, when so many fields are ideologically charged, especially in the social sciences and humanities where there are sharp differences over methodology and result, the difficulties of the process are compounded. An attempt to show someone the door is almost bound to be regarded as a political move. And not in just the trivial sense of the term, which means that people disagree, but rather in its "hard" sense. Matters are made worse when it is held that truth is a variable social construct connected to the interests and ideologies of particular groups.

I don't know whether a case against Anthony Martin could be sustained. He believes his position to be correct, but perhaps it could be shown that he is indifferent or professionally negligent with regard to the contrary evidence. Showing indifference or negligence with regard to the truth, both forms of "professional incompetency," seems to be crucial. For otherwise all professors could be in trouble, since they at least occasionally make false statements in class. On the other hand, a knowing, deliberate falsehood, absent special circumstances, is a grave academic sin.

Yet it is important to be clear on what the case against Professor Martin would be. Is the case that he teaches falsehoods as truths? Or is it that he apparently teaches (or even preaches) anti-Semitism, however sanitized? There is a difference between them. The former, assuming it could be established, would be academic misconduct; the latter, that his opinions are deplorable, even detestable and dangerous. And it would seem that it is the latter that Professor Matsuda finds troubling about sanitized racism and sanitized anti-Semitism.

But it is precisely the expression of deplorable opinions and theses that academic freedom and the principle of campus free speech protect—not just garden variety controversial opinions but also deplorable opinions. Of course, the two types are sometimes hard to distinguish. It is probably the case that opinions that we think are deplorable, whether evaluative or theoretical, rest on or involve claims that we think are false. The reader is invited to pick his or her own favorite deplorable opinions to see if this assertion is correct.

In my view universities are rife with all sorts of deplorable opinions and theses being taught these days. I wish that they could be kept out but I don't see how they can, once they are there, except by constant criticism leading to their demise. Universities unfortunately are sanctuaries for academic cranks, crackpots, and charlatans, who have a kind of "phony's privilege." They end up controlling academic discourse to a degree because of the constant necessity of refuting them.

I tend to think, then, that detenuring a Professor Martin is a virtual nonstarter. While it might not be impossible, I conclude that a university can't get rid of a sanitized racist or anti-Semite very easily. The kind of "discipline" to which he may be subjected is the standard one: critical examination and refutation of his beliefs. It may also be important to publicize the critical examination to the whole campus.

Would this be enough? The "vulnerable" students who come to Wellesley disposed toward anti-Semitism will likely have their prejudices strengthened, and critical examination might not be enough to overcome them. An official statement to the effect that the college disapproves of Professor Martin's teachings might have some positive effect on students, but it puts the administration in the position of taking sides on what at least *seems* to be an intellectual controversy. To that extent, doing so is a risky matter that could pose a danger to academic freedom—but isn't that what speech codes do? Would the denial of a merit raise be appropriate? No professor is automatically entitled to one. As against Anthony Martin it might be an appropriate sanction, but only insofar as it is based on scholarly and pedagogical considerations. As for the vulnerable students, at least those disposed toward Martin's views, it is more likely to create resentment and strengthen their prejudices.

In a case such as this, then, there may be no alternative to the "discipline" of critical examination and refutation. I wonder what Professor Matsuda would propose.

There are, as we know from just reading the newspapers, many people who do think that expression of demeaning ideas should be a punishable campus offense.

At a news conference on September 10, 1997, Professor Lino Graglia of the University of Texas (Austin) Law School stepped into the pressure cooker of the affirmative action debate on the campus. His opposition to affirmative action was well known—in 1976 he published a book *Disaster by Decree: The Supreme Court Decisions on Race and the Schools*. At the news conference he stated that black and Mexican American students are not academically competitive with white and Asian students at the nation's top universities. Characteristically, the reference to Asian students was dropped from newspaper reports. When pressed by a reporter as to whether he thought the cause was "genetic or cultural," Graglia said that the minority students' inability to compete "is the result primarily of cultural effects. . . . They have a culture that seems not to encourage achievement. Failure is not looked upon with disgrace." In response to Graglia, a former UT student wondered "whether he has a white robe and hood hidden in his closet."[36]

But this wasn't the worst of it. At a rally protesting the *Hopwood* decision (which declared affirmative action at the University of Texas Law School to be unlawful),[37] the Reverend Jesse Jackson urged students to treat Graglia as "a moral and social pariah," as a punishment for what Jackson called his "racist, fascist, offensive speech." Fifty professors at the law school wrote a letter condemning Graglia's remarks and the NAACP accused him of "racial harassment." Students and state lawmakers called for Professor Graglia's dismissal. Because Graglia was tenured he couldn't be dismissed, and in any case the administration agreed that Graglia couldn't be dismissed just because of his expression of a highly controversial view.[38]

Whatever his faculty status is, it is doubtful that Professor Matsuda could support any "discipline" for Professor Graglia stronger than condemnation of his views by the administration of the university. For Matsuda holds that proclaiming the superiority of one race over another is permitted as long as the message isn't hateful and persecutory.[39] It is true that she states this in connection with her proposal to criminalize "racial propaganda," while the university "raises unique concerns" because of the vulnerability of students. Still, in saying that black and Mexican American students are not competitive with white and Asian students for cultural reasons, Graglia did not proclaim the superiority of one race over another, as he arguably would have done had he explained the cause of the academic differences as genetic rather than cultural.

There is a more crucial question here: whether there can be an open discussion at the University of Texas of affirmative action in law school and university admissions and what the terms of that debate should be. It is true that in the course of that debate remarks may be made that black and Mexican American students *take* to be demeaning, but if someone is punished for them how open will that debate be? Plainly, not all sides will be heard and not all the issues will be explored.

In any event, the cases of Martin and Graglia are not identical. The former involved in-class expression and the latter out-of-class but on-campus expression.[40] It is therefore doubtful anyway that Graglia could be charged with academic misconduct—Graglia has taught at the Texas law school for over thirty years, with a clean record on his dealings with students of different races and ethnicity. He would probably defend himself by denying that he is Professor Matsuda's "dead-wrong" social scientist; his assertions, he would say, are true, and that in fact there are some social scientists (including blacks) who agree with him.[41] Even if his statements are demeaning of black and Mexican American students, detenuring him doesn't—and shouldn't—stand much of a chance. Again, critical examination seems the only alternative.

Tenure protects the Graglias of this world as much as it protects the Martins. Nontenured faculty who express controversial or provocative ideas will not be protected unless there is a strong commitment to free speech on campus. Students need the same kind of commitment.

I have tried to present the critical race theorists' arguments for speech codes as sympathetically as I can. In fact, I do have some sympathy for their position—not because I find the arguments overwhelming, but rather because racial slurs and racist ideas are loathsome. As I have acknowledged, the arguments are not without some force, but I find them generally to be problematic. Their speech-restrictive conclusions strike me as a threat to the exchange of ideas; if it weren't for that I might be more inclined to support prohibitions on slurs and epithets. We have already seen adoption of their proposals on many American campuses. I don't think that the university is a more hospitable place as a result. And an atmosphere exists on the campus in which the discussion of controversial subjects has become difficult.

The arguments of the critical race theorists for speech restrictions by and large focuses on race and sometimes religion and ethnicity. Rather similar arguments have been made regarding a variety of groups, e.g., women and homosexuals. In my view, the most powerful arguments regarding the American scene are those concerning blacks. And if these do not succeed, as I maintain, then they are unlikely to succeed for others.

HOSTILE ENVIRONMENT AND VERBAL HARASSMENT

Professor Alan M. Dershowitz, of the Harvard Law School, recounts the following experience when teaching the law of rape in a course on criminal law. He spent two days discussing false reports of rape and presented arguments for disclosing the names of complaining witnesses. A small group of feminist students in the class threatened to bring charges of "hostile-environment sexual harassment" against him. Although these students eventually decided against bringing the charges, Dershowitz found it unthinkable that at a major university the teaching of a controversial issue might constitute hostile-environment sexual harassment. "Despite the fact that the vast majority of students wanted to hear all sides of important issues regarding the law of rape," he says, "a small minority tried to use the law of sexual harassment as a tool of censorship."[42]

How might such a situation arise? Does the embodiment of the law of verbal sexual harassment in speech codes pose a threat to campus speech?

We noted in chapter 1 that three basic models of speech codes have been identified: the fighting words approach, the emotional distress theory, and the nondiscrimination/harassment option. Perhaps it can be said that the three writers we have been discussing represent, in greater or lesser degree, all three of these models; but the Stanford code, though it purports to be a fighting words approach, in fact emphasizes the nondiscrimination/harassment option. Although we have already discussed the pitfalls of the Stanford policy, more needs to be said about this aspect. As mentioned above, it appears to adopt language from federal law on workplace harassment.

In the discussion that follows we shall not be concerned with the law of workplace harassment as such; it is a very large topic. There is no doubt in my mind that harassment, sexual or otherwise, can be a serious problem in the workplace and that it can cause harm. Our concern, rather, is with its appropriation by campus speech and conduct codes. Because we have already dealt with many of the issues by implication, the discussion that follows will be relatively brief.

A bit of history, first. Title VII of the Civil Rights Act of 1964 generally made it unlawful for an employer to discriminate in hiring, in firing, and in terms and conditions of employment on the basis of race, color, religion, sex, or national origin. An employer who thus discriminated could be held liable for damages.

Initially, however, the term "discrimination" was not defined. Definition was in effect the work of the Equal Employment Opportunity Commission (EEOC), which was charged with the Act's enforcement, and the courts. Sexual harassment was construed by the EEOC to be a form of discrimination. Its guidelines provide the commonly accepted definition of "sexual harassment," adapted by the courts to racial harassment:

> [V]erbal or physical conduct of a sexual nature [that] has the purpose or effect of unreasonably interfering with an individual's work performance or creating an intimidating, hostile, or offensive working environment.[43]

This definition is widely used also by state and local agencies as well as courts, which have ruled on numerous cases of sexual harassment. (There appear to be far fewer cases on racial harassment.) In 1986, the Supreme Court added the limitation that to be actionable the conduct must be sufficiently "severe or pervasive" to alter the conditions of the victim's employment.[44] This limitation seems frequently to be overlooked by many writers but especially by people bringing charges of sexual harassment.[45] Sexual harassment has been said to be the "whiplash injury" of the nineties. How such harassment *necessarily* is a form of discrimination is not clear to me, but this is how things worked out.[46]

It is pretty clear from whence campus regulations on "verbal discriminatory harassment" are derived. Although educational institutions were not covered by the 1964 Act, Title IX of the Education Amendments, in 1972, outlawed discrimination on the basis of sex in educational institutions receiving federal dollars, which could be lost if an institution fails to ensure that its campus is not a hostile environment for women and minorities. Department of Education regulations also make universities liable for harassment by faculty members, employees, students, and even guest speakers, that is "sufficiently severe, pervasive, and persistent so as to interfere with or limit the ability of an individual to participate in or benefit from" the services and activities of an educational program.

It should be noted that sexual harassment law places liability on the employer and not on the employee. Prudent employers are therefore advised to adopt workplace rules that will minimize the occurrence of harassment, which may result in restrictions on speech that the government itself could not impose. For instance, in order to ensure that an employee will not feel harassed on religious grounds—which Title VII also forbids—by someone distributing religious tracts in the office or plant, the employer might forbid their distribution. The government, on the other hand, could not do this. In general, employers may find it in their interests to go beyond what hostile-environment law requires, even to "zero tolerance," in order to be on the safe side. They may find it in their interest to forbid all sexual expression. Various commentators understandably argue that the EEOC guidelines raise First Amendment questions, which have been sidestepped by the courts.[47] While employers presumably could, on their own, restrict religious or sexual expression in their own workplaces, e.g., forbid the placement of a *Hustler* centerfold on the wall, First Amendment questions arise when they restrict or penalize an employee because of the government's threat of liability. First Amendment questions arise, furthermore, because of the standard reasons: the vagueness, content-based, and viewpoint non-neutrality of the guidelines. Critics of workplace harassment law cannot be simply dismissed, as one radical feminist has done, as millions of men who want a young woman to "suck their cock."[48]

But even if the EEOC guidelines are constitutional, as is assumed in the Supreme Court's jurisprudence, their adaptation to the university context still is questionable.[49] The workplace has been described as a place for "getting the job done," and the prohibition of harassment, sexual or otherwise, that is "sufficiently severe or pervasive to alter the conditions of the victim's employment" could be acceptable on efficiency criteria alone. Though even then, it might be a mistake to put all workplaces in one basket.

The university is a place for the transmission and promotion of knowledge. Inevitably, in the university, controversial ideas will be presented and debated, and harassment guidelines from the industrial or business workplace may put a damper on the university's function. Because of this, neither a public nor a private university (unless an exception should be made for openly sectarian institutions) should discipline students or faculty on the basis of content or viewpoint of speech.

This consideration is somewhat honored in the Department of Education's (DOE) guidelines for the investigation of discrimination cases under Title IX. These guidelines declare that "Title IX is intended to protect students from sex discrimination, not to regulate the content of speech." This point is made clear by Norma V. Cantu, assistant secretary for civil rights of the DOE, in a letter published in the *New York Times*. She was responding to an article that cited the chancellor of the University of Massachusetts as saying that DOE regulations require the institution of a speech code. "[T]here are no . . . regulations that endorse or prescribe speech codes," she says. The guidance of the Office of Civil Rights explicitly states that "O.C.R. cannot endorse or prescribe speech or conduct codes or other campus policies to the extent that they violate the First Amendment to the United States Constitution."[50] (What else could it say?)

It is for this reason that the DOE has modified the EEOC guidelines for investigating sexual and racial harassment claims. Whereas the EEOC forbids "verbal conduct" that has the "purpose or effect of . . . creating an intimidating, hostile, or offensive working environment," the DOE drops the words "intimidating" and "offensive." For racial harassment it bans a "hostile environment," and for sexual harassment it bans a "hostile or abusive educational environment." These changes seem to have been made in recognition of the speech-code cases that ruled it impermissible to ban speech because someone finds it offensive. A number of schools, however, have adopted with little or no modification the EEOC's guidelines on hostile-environment sexual harassment.[51]

It is not surprising that they should have done so, despite Ms. Cantu's assurances. For to avoid liability under Title IX, universities have an incentive to monitor sexual expression in the fashion of business employers.[52] Employment lawyers maintain that sexual harassment may include sexual propositions, sexual innuendo, suggestive comments, sexually oriented kidding, and practical jokes. And just as employers may avoid liability by adopting anti-harassment policies that monitor speech, so might universities find it in their interest to do so, too. Verbal sexual harassment and hostile environment are such vague notions that even sending a dirty joke on one's private computer, or leaving a porno site open on it in a dormitory room could (and probably already has) become policed. The potential for intrusion (by monitoring e-mail and computer files, as many employers do) is alarming.

I don't mean to make a brief for dirty jokes or for pornography. And I don't mean to minimize the awfulness of sexual harassment, especially that of the quid pro quo variety. It is of course generally a terrible thing for someone to be in a hostile or abusive environment. And so is it for someone to be harassed in the ordinary sense of the term, that is, to be subjected to deliberate pestering and disturbance by unwelcome speech or action. Constantly playing one's radio loudly in order to disturb is an example. Such speech and action should be covered by a campus conduct code.

But the problem with the hostile-environment concept for academic institutions remains. The concept, like that of offense and intimidation, poses a threat to free speech and inquiry—and it is this threat that is our prime worry. Controversial ideas are put forward in a variety of courses and fields: philosophy, psychology, law, biology, and so on. The statistics professor who questions some claim made about female employment, the social work student who says he considers homosexuality a treatable disease, the college student who disputes multiculturalism, the male medical student who says that women shouldn't become surgeons, the biology professor who maintains . . . it's easy to fill in the blanks. The expression of an idea can be—and has been—viewed as hostile and sexually or racially harassing, as Professor Dershowitz discovered. What is particularly of concern is that many professors are hesitant even to take up controversial subjects and many students are hesitant to take controversial stands, as I have been told by individuals from different fields.

Although we haven't come (yet) to see it instituted, the nadir, the bottom of the slippery slope, of hostile-environment discriminatory harassment is the idea of "anti-feminist *intellectual* harassment." At the 1991 meeting of the Modern Language Association Annette Kolodny, a former dean at the University of Arizona, was asked to define this notion as a specific category of discrimination for a forum on Anti-feminist Harassment in the Academy. She suggested the following:

> Anti-feminist intellectual harassment, a serious threat to academic freedom, occurs when (1) any policy, action, statement, and/or behavior has the intent or effect of discouraging or preventing women's freedom of lawful action, freedom of thought, and freedom of expression; (2) *or* when any policy, action, statement, and/or behavior creates an environment in which the appropriate application of feminist theories or methodologies to research, scholarship, and teaching is devalued, discouraged, or altogether thwarted; (3) *or* when any policy, action, statement, and/or behavior creates an environment in which research, scholarship, and teaching pertaining to women, gender, or gender inequities is devalued, discouraged, or altogether thwarted.

On this sweeping definition, any criticism of feminism could be perceived as harassment, since it could be perceived as devaluing or discouraging it. There are, to be sure, feminists who criticize other feminists, but if Professor Kolodny were their dean they would have cause for concern. If feminism involves ideas, so does criticism of feminism. (Just imagine a prohibition on anti-capitalist intellectual harassment.) And all this is said by her to be in defense of academic freedom.[53]

Of course there are defenders of speech and harassment codes who are worried about the possibility of overreaching and the restricting of the expression of controversial ideas. We can put aside the far-out sorts of restrictions that have been mentioned earlier in these chapters.[54] As we saw in the case of the Stanford policy, some codes nod in the direction of free speech principles. Others are more affirmative and also include the "severe and pervasive" requirement as well. The Duke University policy on harassment is a good example:

> Duke University is committed to protecting the academic freedom and freedom of expression of all members of the university community. This policy against harassment shall be applied in a manner that protects the academic freedom and freedom of expression of all parties to a complaint. Academic freedom and freedom of expression include, but are not limited to, the expression of ideas, however controversial, in the classroom, in residence halls, and, in keeping with different responsibilities, in work places elsewhere in the university community.

Harassment at Duke is

> A. The creation of a hostile or intimidating environment, in which verbal or physical conduct, because of its severity and/or persistence, is likely to interfere significantly

with an individual's work or education, or affect adversely an individual's living conditions.
(Part B. deals with quid pro quo harassment.)[55]

Duke's is certainly one of the more speech-protective codes, in that it insists
that the "policy against harassment shall be applied in a manner that protects the
academic freedom and freedom of expression of all parties to a complaint." It is
also apparently the case that one instance of hostile speech would not amount to
harassment unless it is "severe."

In this latter respect the Duke policy seems different from Stanford's, which lacks
this requirement. Under the Stanford policy single acts of speech that fit the definition of "harassment by vilification" are presumably punishable whether severe or
not. In this regard, the ban on verbal harassment on the campus appears to be more
restrictive of speech than in the workplace. Thomas Grey states the following:

> [The] injury of discriminatory denial of educational access through maintenance of
> a hostile environment can arise from single acts of discrimination on the part of many
> individuals. To deal with a form of abuse that is repetitive to its victims, and hence
> constitutes the continuing injury of harassment to them, it is necessary to prohibit the
> individual actions that, when added up, amount to institutional discrimination.[56]

On this point, as Eugene Volokh remarks, "Professor Grey is absolutely right: To
avoid the risk of a hostile environment, an institution can't, in practice, just
restate the severity/pervasiveness test—it must 'prohibit the individual actions
[including speech] that, when added up, amount' to a hostile environment."[57]

Of course, the basic difference between Duke's policy and Stanford's lies in the
fact that Duke deliberately chose not to adopt a code-like formulation, with its
series of provisions on verbal harassment or "harassment by vilification." Professor Grey thought that the Stanford code protected campus speech to the extent
it is compatible with the aim of eliminating discriminatory harassment, but we
have found the policy to be problematic. Duke, instead, adopted a broad statement of principle. This means that alleged violations will have to be adjudicated
on a case-by-case basis, which allows for flexibility and fact-sensitivity. Of
course, there are dangers in such an approach.[58] Still, Duke's policy allows for the
development of a campus "common law" of harassment. A further distinction
between the two policies is that Duke rejects the "discriminatory harassment"
option. It prohibits the creation of a hostile or intimidating environment that is
likely to interfere significantly with *any* individual's work or education, or affect
adversely *any* individual's living conditions. This approach is much fairer, a definite plus in my opinion.

Of course, whether Duke's "severity and/or persistence" requirement has real
significance depends on how strong its commitment is to applying its policy "in
a manner that protects the academic freedom and freedom of expression of all
parties to a complaint."

This commitment is crucial, no matter how tightly drafted speech or verbal
harassment codes are. As the Duke University Law School's "Rules, Policies, and

Procedures" states: "Such rules often convey their own intolerance without meaning to do so. However artfully drawn, they can chill a good deal of provocative expression that is altogether desirable."[59] I think we are better off without such codes, but the commitment is indispensable in any case.

NOTES

1. "Public Response to Racist Speech: Considering the Victim's Story," 87 *Michigan Law Rev.* (1989), 2320–81. This article is reprinted in M. J. Matsuda, C. R. Lawrence III, R. Delgado, and K. W. Crenshaw, *Words That Wound: Critical Race Theory, Assaultive Speech and the First Amendment* (Boulder, Colo.: Westview Press, 1993), 17–52.

2. *Words That Wound*, 17.

3. *Words That Wound*, 27.

4. *Words That Wound*, 23.

5. *Words That Wound*, 35.

6. *Words That Wound*, 36.

7. *Words That Wound*, 36.

8. *Words That Wound*, 40.

9. *Words That Wound*, 40.

10. *Words That Wound*, 41.

11. *Words That Wound*, 44.

12. *Words That Wound*, 44.

13. [1990] 3 R.C.S. 697.

14. For an analysis of the majority and dissenting opinions, see Lorraine E. Weinrib, "Hate Promotion in a Free and Democratic Society," 36 *McGill Law J.* 1416–49 (1991). See also Weinrib's contribution to the Hate Speech Symposium in 6 *Touro International Law Rev.* (1995), 9-32 ("Comparison of Rights Protection under the U.S. Constitution and Under the Canadian *Charter of Rights and Freedoms*"). Professor Weinrib favors the majority's view. It seems to me, as an outsider, that a number of Canadian provinces have made serious inroads into the freedom of speech, going beyond restrictions on "hate promotion."

15. See chapter 4, n. 33.

16. *Board of Education v. Pico*, 457 U.S. 853 (1982). The nine books in question included *Slaughter House Five*, by Kurt Vonnegut, Jr. and *Black Boy*, by Richard Wright.

17. *Board of Education v. Pico*, at 882.

18. *Board of Education v. Pico*, at 909 and 914.

19. *Sweezy v. New Hampshire*, 354 U.S. 234 (1957). See text, chapter 3, at n. 11.

20. *Rust et al. v. Sullivan*, 500 U.S. 173 (1990), at 200. The *Rust* case concerned a challenge to Department of Health and Human Services regulations that limited the abortion-related activities of certain individuals.

21. See "In a Revolution of Rules, Campuses Go Full Circle," *New York Times*, March 3, 1999, A1. The trend back toward *in loco parentis* is not just about the need for rules; it fits in with other cultural phenomena, the recovery movement, education for self-esteem, and the state as the ultimate therapist.

22. Rodney A. Smolla, "Academic Freedom, Hate Speech, and the Idea of a University," 53 *Law and Contemporary Problems* (Summer 1990), 195–226.

23. A hard case to classify is that of Arthur R. Butz, a professor of electrical and computer engineering at Northwestern University. His Holocaust-denial Web site, he says,

"exists for expressing views outside the purview of my role as an Electrical Engineering faculty member" (http://pubweb.acns.nwu.edu/~abutz/). This site, however, appears to be in the Northwestern Web system and is therefore presumably on-campus. Off-campus statements would have First Amendment protection, though some might argue that when they are claimed to fall under a professor's professional expertise they are protected by his academic freedom, too.

24. Or harassing. Compare the situation of Professor Dershowitz, at n. 42, below.

25. The main *Boston Globe* articles are: April 7, 1993, 26 ("Jewish groups rap Wellesley professor"); April 9, 1993, 19 ("Afro-centrist Wellesley professor rejects charges he is anti-Semitic"); April 13, 1993, 18 ("Hate literature as history"); January 29, 1994, 21 ("At Wellesley, a war of words"); February 24, 1994, 51 ("Teaching history or hate"); March 17, 1994, 29 ("Wellesley faculty joins book protest"); August 26, 1994, 23 ("Wellesley denies raise to professor"); September 27, 1994, 1 ("Black academics split on Afrocentrism").

26. *The Secret Relationship between Blacks and Jews* (Chicago: Latimer Associates, 1991). This book is produced by the Historical Research Department of the Nation of Islam.

27 *Secret Relationship,* vii.

28. Martin responded with a book, *The Jewish Onslaught: Dispatches from the Wellesley Battlefront* (Dover, Mass.: Majority Press, 1993), describing what Martin calls "dirty Jewish tricks" against him and also criticizing individual faculty members and the college's administration. The president of the college denied Martin another merit increase. In a letter to 40,000 alumnae, parents, and friends, President Walsh defended Martin's right to free speech "without fear of reprisals" but also denounced the book's "recurrent and gratuitous use of racial or religious identification of individuals" and its attempt to portray Wellesley College as a "repressive institution bent on silencing him." Martin, she said, "crossed the line" between "simply unpopular argument" and "unnecessarily disrespectful and deeply divisive speech." (*Boston Globe*, January 29, 1994, 21.) The president's intervention attracted some debate. The civil libertarian Nat Hentoff thought the letter was an appropriate exercise of the president's free speech rights. The civil libertarians Kors and Silverglate criticized it, because it attaches conditions to the right to free speech "without fear of reprisals." See their discussion of the incident in A. C. Kors and H. A. Silverglate, *The Shadow University: The Betrayal of Liberty on America's Campuses* (New York: Free Press, 1998), 104–7.

29. See Harold Brackman, *Ministry of Lies: The Truth behind the Nation of Islam's "The Secret Relationship between Blacks and Jews"* (New York: Four Walls Eight Windows, 1994); Eli Faber, *Jews, Slaves, and the Slave Trade: Setting the Record Straight* (New York: New York University Press, 1998). Selwyn Cudjoe, the chairman of Martin's department, condemned the book as "patently and scurrilously anti-Semitic" and many black scholars agree with this assessment (*Boston Globe*, April 7, 1993, 26).

30. Would it be wrong to assign statements in defense of slavery by pre-Civil War planters, in an American history course? I've heard that a Harvard professor who suffered abuse for having done so was forced to cancel his course.

31. See the discussion in chapter 3.

32. *Feldman v. Ho*, 171 F.3d 494 (7th Cir. 1999), at 495. Southern Illinois University decided in 1990 not to renew the contract of Marcus Feldman, an assistant professor of mathematics in his fourth year of teaching. The case involved Feldman's claim that his First Amendment rights were violated when his contract was not renewed because of his accusation that a colleague had committed academic misconduct by plagiarizing a schol-

arly paper. The university investigated the accusation and vindicated the colleague. The court's ruling is that the quality judgment that Feldman's contract should not be renewed is one that belongs to the University to make, and not to a jury on the grounds that his freedom of speech was violated, for then "we might as well commit all tenure decisions to juries, for all are equally based on speech" (at 497).

33. Ibid., citing *Feldman v. Bahn*, 12 F.3d (1993), at 732–33 (emphasis in original).

34. See appendix A, 53 *Law and Contemporary Problems* (Summer 1990), 406. There is a large literature on academic tenure; this issue of the journal contains a number of useful articles and references.

35. Cited in *Law and Contemporary Problems*, 325, from William W. Van Alstyne, "Tenure: A Summary, Explanation, and 'Defense,'" 57 *AAUP Bull.* 328 (1971) (emphasis in original).

36. These quotations come from a Web site that collects materials on affirmative action and diversity: http:// humanitas.ucsb.edu/projects/aa.

37. *Hopwood v. Texas*, 78 F.3d 932 (5th Cir. 1996).

38. See Lisa Tozzi, "Gagging Graglia," *Austin Chronicle*, February 9, 1998 (found at http://weeklywire.com/WW/02-02-98/austin_pols_feature3.html). Many exchanges on Graglia may be found in contemporary issues of *Chronicle of Higher Education*.

39. See text at n. 6.

40. Compare with these the cases of Professor Michael Levin and Professor Leonard Jeffries, both of the City College in New York. Levin's provocative statements (about blacks) were made in printed articles and letters, and Jeffries's (about Jews) were made at an off-campus symposium. Levin claimed that the average black is less intelligent than the average white; Jeffries that Jews were engaged in a conspiracy for the destruction of blacks. The college "disciplined" them: shadow sections of one of Levin's courses were created, so that students were not forced to have him as a teacher; Jeffries's chairmanship of the black studies program was curtailed. Both sued on various grounds (including free speech) and both won. For an account, see Robert M. O'Neil, *Free Speech in the College Community* (Bloomington: Indiana University Press, 1997), 31–42.

41. A National Task Force on Minority High Achievement was formed in 1997 by the College Board to investigate why the academic achievement of black middle-class and upper-income high school students lags behind whites of comparable socioeconomic status. See *New York Times*, July 4, 1999, sec. 1, 1: "Reason is Sought for Lag in Blacks in School Effort." The role of cultural factors is suggested in the article.

42. See www.vix.com/pub/men/harass/dershowitz.html. The students may have thought they had a case because the Harvard Law School Sexual Harassment Guidelines prohibit "speech or conduct of a sexual nature." Other provisions of the guidelines apparently show that they were mistaken to think so. See, for details, www.law.harvard.edu/Administrative_Services/Personnel/harassment.html.

43. Cited from 29 C.F.R. § 1604.11(a)(3) in Kingsley R. Browne," Title VII as Censorship: Hostile-Environment Harassment and the First Amendment," 52 *Ohio State Law J.* (1991), 482, n. 8. The EEOC guidelines also make unlawful "quid pro quo" harassment, where submission to unwelcome sexual advances or requests is an explicit or implicit term or condition of employment or where submission or rejection of the conduct is used as a basis for an employment decision. Quid pro quo harassment is a form of extortion, and employers may be held "strictly liable" for such harassment by supervisors. We are concerned only with hostile-environment harassment as defined in the text. Quid pro quo harassment is further reflected in campus regulations that restrict, or require disclosure of, intimate personal relations between faculty members and students.

44. *Meritor Savings Bank v. Vinson*, 477 U.S. 57, 67 (1986) (even if unwelcome sexual demands were not linked to specific employment benefits, sexual harassment that is "sufficiently severe or pervasive" to create a "hostile or abusive work environment" gives rise to liability).

45. See Eugene Volokh, "What Speech Does 'Hostile Work Environment' Harassment Law Restrict?," 85 *Georgetown Law J.* (1997), 627–48.

46. The argument seems to be that because sexual harassment is primarily a problem for women, it is a form of discrimination. See Catharine MacKinnon, *The Sexual Harassment of Working Women* (New Haven: Yale University Press, 1979). MacKinnon, a radical feminist, locates sexuality in a theory of gender inequality, so that even consensual sex can constitute discrimination. For a criticism, see Daphne Patai, *Heterophobia* (Lanham, Md.: Rowman & Littlefield, 1998), especially chapter 7. We cannot go into the issue here.

47. See the article by Kingsley R. Browne, cited at n. 43, 481–547. There is a very large literature, pro and con, on the subject.

48. Attributed to Andrea Dworkin in Jeffrey Rosen, "In Defense of Gender-Blindness," *The New Republic*, June 29, 1998, 25. Recall that the notion of sexual harassment has been debated in the general media because of the allegations of Paula Jones and Kathleen Willey against President Clinton.

49. See the helpful article by Robert W. Gall, "The University as an Industrial Plant: How a Workplace Theory of Discriminatory Harassment Creates a 'Hostile Environment' for Free Speech in America's Universities," 60 *Law and Contemporary Problems* (Autumn 1997), 203–43.

50. Letter to the Editor, December 8, 1995, A30.

51. For citations and a discussion of the modifications, see Gall, 229–31. Gall's article provides an analysis of policies on harassment at six academic institutions.

52. On May 24, 1999, a divided (5–4) Supreme Court decided the case of *Davis v. Monroe County Board of Education* (No. 97-843). It held that a public school may be held liable in damages for student-on-student sexual harassment where it is deliberately indifferent to known sexual harassment that is "so severe, pervasive, and objectively offensive that it can be said to deprive the victims of access to the educational opportunities or benefits provided by the school" (per Justice O'Connor, 67 *U.S. Law Week* 4329, at 4335). It is hard to know how far this holding goes. Of particular interest to us is part of the *dissenting* opinion: "Perhaps even more startling than its broad assumptions about school control over primary and secondary school students is the majority's failure to grapple in any meaningful way with the distinction between elementary and secondary schools, on the one hand, and universities on the other. . . . Yet the majority's holding would appear to apply with equal force to universities, which do not exercise custodial and tutelary power over their adult students. A university's power to discipline its students for speech that may constitute sexual harassment is also circumscribed by the First Amendment. . . . The difficulties associated with speech codes simply underscore the limited nature of a university's control over student behavior that may be viewed as sexual harassment" (per Justice Kennedy, at 4340).

53. Quoted from Annette Kolodny, *Failing the Future: A Dean Looks at Higher Education in the Twenty-First Century* (Durham, N.C.: Duke University Press, 1998), 105 (italics in original), in Patai, *Heterophobia*, 188. See, also, "New Project on Antifeminist Harassment, *MLA Newsletter,* September, 1991, 21. As Professor Patai points out, her own book might be an instance of antifeminist intellectual harassment.

54. Some of these far-out restrictions are to be found in guidebooks and manuals on harassment written for college administrators. For a critical account, see Patai, *Heterophobia*.

55. 1997–98 Bulletin of Duke University: Information and Regulations, 63; see www.duke.edu/web/equity/har_pol.htm, for further details.

56. Thomas C. Grey, "How to Write a Speech Code Without Really Trying: Reflections on the Stanford Experience," 29 *U.C. Davis L. Rev.* 891–956 (1996), at 902.

57. Volokh, 646 (brackets in original).

58. See Gall, 238: "Even when Duke or another university modifies hostile environment theory in such a way that, on its face, its harassment policy avoids the evils of prohibiting speech because of disagreement with the ideas it contains or its perceived offensiveness, 'hostile environment' theory creates a fuzzy, prohibited zone of speech of which teachers and students must steer clear if they are not to be punished. Too much discretion is invested in those who, with the best of intentions, may choose to use the policies to ban speech which they believe offends 'enlightened' sensibilities."

59. Duke University Law School's "Rules, Policies, and Procedures," www.law.duke.edu/general/info/s11.html#policy11-5 (Dean's Statement on Freedom of Expression in the Law School).

Appendix A

John Doe v. University of Michigan

721 F.SUPP. 852 (1989)
SEPT. 22, 1989; ADDENDUM SEPT. 25, 1989
OPINION (ABRIDGED; SAVED FOOTNOTES RENUMBERED)

COHN, District Judge.

I. INTRODUCTION

It is an unfortunate fact of our constitutional system that the ideals of freedom and equality are often in conflict. The difficult and sometimes painful task of our political and legal institutions is to mediate the appropriate balance between these two competing values. Recently, the University of Michigan at Ann Arbor (the University), a state-chartered university, see Mich. Const. art. VIII, adopted a Policy on Discrimination and Discriminatory Harassment of Students in the University Environment (the Policy) in an attempt to curb what the University's governing Board of Regents (Regents) viewed as a rising tide of racial intolerance and harassment on campus. The Policy prohibited individuals, under the penalty of sanctions, from "stigmatizing or victimizing" individuals or groups on the basis of race, ethnicity, religion, sex, sexual orientation, creed, national origin, ancestry, age, marital status, handicap or Vietnam-era veteran status. However laudable or appropriate an effort this may have been, the Court found that the Policy swept within its scope a significant amount of "verbal conduct" or "verbal behavior" which is unquestionably protected speech under the First Amendment. Accordingly, the Court granted plaintiff John Doe's (Doe) prayer for a permanent injunction as to those parts of the Policy restricting speech activity, but denied the injunction as to the Policy's regulation of physical conduct. The reasons follow.

95

II. FACTS GENERALLY [OMITTED]

III. THE UNIVERSITY OF MICHIGAN POLICY ON DISCRIMINATION AND DISCRIMINATORY HARASSMENT

A. The Terms of the Policy

The Policy established a three-tiered system whereby the degree of regulation was dependent on the location of the conduct at issue. The broadest range of speech and dialogue was "tolerated" in variously described public parts of the campus. Only an act of physical violence or destruction of property was considered sanctionable in these settings. Publications sponsored by the University such as the Michigan Daily and the Michigan Review were not subject to regulation. The conduct of students living in University housing is primarily governed by the standard provisions of individual leases, however the Policy appeared to apply in this setting as well. The Policy by its terms applied specifically to "[e]ducational and academic centers, such as classroom buildings, libraries, research laboratories, recreation and study centers[.]" In these areas, persons were subject to discipline for:

1. Any behavior, verbal or physical, that stigmatizes or victimizes an individual on the basis of race, ethnicity, religion, sex, sexual orientation, creed, national origin, ancestry, age, marital status, handicap or Vietnam-era veteran status, and that
   a. Involves an express or implied threat to an individual's academic efforts, employment, participation in University sponsored extra-curricular activities or personal safety; or
   b. Has the purpose or reasonably foreseeable effect of interfering with an Individual's academic efforts, employment, participation in University sponsored extra-curricular activities or personal safety; or
   c. Creates an intimidating, hostile, or demeaning environment for educational pursuits, employment or participation in University sponsored extra-curricular activities.
2. Sexual advances, requests for sexual favors, and verbal or physical conduct that stigmatizes or victimizes an individual on the basis of sex or sexual orientation where such behavior:
   a. Involves an express or implied threat to an individual's academic efforts, employment, participation in University sponsored extra-curricular activities or personal safety; or
   b. Has the purpose or reasonably foreseeable effect of interfering with an individual's academic efforts, employment, participation in University sponsored extra-curricular activities or personal safety; or
   c. Creates an intimidating, hostile, or demeaning environment for educational pursuits, employment or participation in University sponsored extra-curricular activities.

On August 22, 1989, the University publicly announced, without prior notice to the Court or Doe, that it was withdrawing section 1(c) on the grounds that "a need exists for further explanation and clarification of [that section] of the policy." No reason was given why the analogous provision in paragraph 2(c) was allowed to stand.

The Policy by its terms recognizes that certain speech which might be considered in violation may not be sanctionable, stating: "The Office of the General Counsel will rule on any claim that conduct which is the subject of a formal hearing is constitutionally protected by the first amendment."

B. Hearing Procedures [Omitted]

C. Sanctions

The Policy provided for progressive discipline based on the severity of the violation. It stated that the University encouraged hearing panels to impose sanctions that include an educational element in order to sensitize the perpetrator to the harmfulness of his or her conduct. The Policy provided, however, that compulsory class attendance should not be imposed "in an attempt to change deeply held religious or moral convictions." Depending on the intent of the accused student, the effect of the conduct, and whether the accused student is a repeat offender, one or more of the following sanctions may be imposed: (1) formal reprimand; (2) community service; (3) class attendance; (4) restitution; (5) removal from University housing; (6) suspension from specific courses and activities; (7) suspension; (8) expulsion. The sanctions of suspension and expulsion could only be imposed for violent or dangerous acts, repeated offenses, or a willful failure to comply with a lesser sanction. The University President could set aside or lessen any sanction.

D. Interpretive Guide

Shortly after the promulgation of the policy in the fall of 1988, the University Office of Affirmative Action issued an interpretive guide (Guide) entitled What Students Should Know about Discrimination and Discriminatory Harassment by Students in the University Environment. The Guide purported to be an authoritative interpretation of the Policy and provided examples of sanctionable conduct. These included:

A flyer containing racist threats distributed in a residence hall.
Racist graffiti written on the door of an Asian student's study carrel.
A male student makes remarks in class like "Women just aren't as good in this field as men," thus creating a hostile learning atmosphere for female classmates.
Students in a residence hall have a floor party and invite everyone on their floor except one person because they think she might be a lesbian.

A black student is confronted and racially insulted by two white students in a cafeteria.

Male students leave pornographic pictures and jokes on the desk of a female graduate student.

Two men demand that their roommate in the residence hall move out and be tested for AIDS.

In addition, the Guide contained a separate section entitled "You are a harasser when . . ." which contains the following examples of discriminatory conduct:

You exclude someone from a study group because that person is of a different race, sex, or ethnic origin than you are.

You tell jokes about gay men and lesbians.

Your student organization sponsors entertainment that includes a comedian who slurs Hispanics.

You display a confederate flag on the door of your room in the residence hall.

You laugh at a joke about someone in your class who stutters.

You make obscene telephone calls or send racist notes or computer messages.

You comment in a derogatory way about a particular person or group's physical appearance or sexual orientation, or their cultural origins, or religious beliefs.

It was not clear whether each of these actions would subject a student to sanctions, although the title of the section suggests that they would. It was also unclear why these additional examples were listed separately from those in the section entitled "What is Discriminatory Harassment."

According to the University, the Guide was withdrawn at an unknown date in the winter of 1989, because "the information in it was not accurate." The withdrawal had not been announced publicly as of the date this case was filed.

IV. STANDING

[1] Doe is a psychology graduate student. His specialty is the field of biopsychology, which he describes as the interdisciplinary study of the biological bases of individual differences in personality traits and mental abilities. Doe said that certain controversial theories positing biologically-based differences between sexes and races might be perceived as "sexist" and "racist" by some students, and he feared that discussion of such theories might be sanctionable under the Policy. He asserted that his right to freely and openly discuss these theories was impermissibly chilled, and he requested that the Policy be declared unconstitutional and enjoined on the grounds of vagueness and overbreadth.

* * *

[As] late as February 2, 1988, the University attorney who researched the law and assisted in the drafting of the Policy, wrote a memorandum in which he conceded that merely offensive speech was constitutionally protected, but declared that

[w]e cannot be frustrated by the reluctance of the courts and the common law to recognize the personal damage that is caused by discriminatory speech, nor should our policy attempt to conform to traditional methods of identifying harmful speech. Rather the University should identify and prohibit that speech that causes damage to individuals within the community.

The record before the Court thus indicated that the drafters of the policy intended that speech need only be offensive to be sanctionable.

The Guide also suggested that the kinds of ideas Doe wished to discuss would be sanctionable. The Guide was the University's authoritative interpretation of the Policy. It explicitly stated that an example of sanctionable conduct would include:

A male student makes remarks in class like "Women just aren't as good in this field as men," thus creating a hostile learning atmosphere for female classmates.

Doe said in an affidavit that he would like to discuss questions relating to sex and race differences in his capacity as a teaching assistant in Psychology 430, Comparative Animal Behavior. He went on to say:

An appropriate topic for discussion in the discussion groups is sexual differences between male and female mammals, including humans. [One] . . . hypothesis regarding sex differences in mental abilities is that men as a group do better than women in some spatially related mental tasks partly because of a biological difference. This may partly explain, for example, why many more men than women chose to enter the engineering profession.

Doe also said that some students and teachers regarded such theories as "sexist" and he feared that he might be charged with a violation of the Policy if he were to discuss them. In light of the statements in the Guide, such fears could not be dismissed as speculative and conjectural. The ideas discussed in Doe's field of study bear sufficient similarity to ideas denounced as "harassing" in the Guide to constitute a realistic and specific threat of prosecution.

The University argued that it had withdrawn the Guide on the grounds that it contained some "inaccuracies." However, at best, this decision was conveyed only to department heads and other responsible officials and, as noted, had not been announced to the general University community at the time this lawsuit was filed. For the purposes of determining Doe's standing, the University's action came too late to render Doe's fear of enforcement illusory. [Citation omitted]

Finally, the record of the University's enforcement of the Policy over the past year suggested that students in the classroom and research setting who offended others by discussing ideas deemed controversial could be and were subject to discipline. A review of the University's discriminatory harassment complaint files suggested that on at least three separate occasions, students were disciplined or threatened with discipline for comments made in a classroom setting. These are discipline files 88-12-21, 88-9-05, and 88-9-07, discussed infra. At least one student was subject to a formal hearing because he stated in the context of a social work research class that he believed that homosexuality was a disease that could be psychologically treated. As will be discussed below, the Policy was enforced so broadly and indiscriminately, that plaintiff's fears of prosecution were entirely reasonable. Accordingly, the Court found that Doe had standing to challenge the policy.

V. VAGUENESS AND OVERBREADTH

* * *

A. Scope of Permissible Regulation

Before inquiring whether the policy is impermissibly vague and overbroad, it would be helpful to first distinguish between verbal conduct and verbal acts that are generally protected by the First Amendment and those that are not. It is the latter class of behavior that the University may legitimately regulate.

Although the line is sometimes difficult to draw with precision, the Court must distinguish at the outset between the First Amendment protection of so-called "pure speech" and mere conduct.
***

While the University's power to regulate so-called pure speech is far more limited, [Citation] certain categories can be generally described as unprotected by the First Amendment.

*** If the Policy had the effect of only regulating in these areas, it is unlikely that any constitutional problem would have arisen.

What the University could not do, however, was establish an anti-discrimination policy which had the effect of prohibiting certain speech because it disagreed with ideas or messages sought to be conveyed. [Citations]
***

Nor could the University proscribe speech simply because it was found to be offensive, even gravely so, by large numbers of people. [Citations]
***

These principles acquire a special significance in the university setting, where the free and unfettered interplay of competing views is essential to the institution's educational mission. [Citations] With these general rules in mind, the Court can now consider whether the Policy sweeps within its scope speech which is otherwise protected by the First Amendment.

B. Overbreadth

[4] Doe claimed that the Policy was invalid because it was facially overbroad. It is fundamental that statutes regulating First Amendment activities must be nar-

rowly drawn to address only the specific evil at hand. [Citations] *** The Supreme Court has consistently held that statutes punishing speech or conduct solely on the grounds that they are unseemly or offensive are unconstitutionally overbroad. [Citations] *** In Papish v. University of Missouri, 410 U.S. 667, 93 S.Ct. 1197, 35 L.Ed.2d 618 (1973), the Supreme Court ordered the reinstatement of a university student expelled for distributing an underground newspaper sporting the headline "Motherfucker acquitted" on the grounds that "the mere dissemination of ideas—no matter how offensive to good taste—on a state university campus may not be shut off in the name alone of conventions of decency." *** Most recently, in Texas v. Johnson, supra, the Supreme Court invalidated a Texas statute prohibiting burning of the American flag on the grounds that there was no showing that the prohibited conduct was likely to incite a breach of the peace. These cases stand generally for the proposition that the state may not prohibit broad classes of speech, some of which may indeed be legitimately regulable, if in so doing a substantial amount of constitutionally protected conduct is also prohibited. This was the fundamental infirmity of the Policy.

The University repeatedly argued that the Policy did not apply to speech that is protected by the First Amendment. It urged the Court to disregard the Guide as "inaccurate" and look instead to "the manner in which the Policy has been interpreted and applied by those charged with its enforcement." However, as applied by the University over the past year, the Policy was consistently applied to reach protected speech.

On December 7, 1988, a complaint was filed against a graduate student in the School of Social Work alleging that he harassed students based on sexual orientation and sex. The basis for the sexual orientation charge was apparently that in a research class, the student openly stated his belief that homosexuality was a disease and that he intended to develop a counseling plan for changing gay clients to straight. See Discipline File 88-12-21, described supra. He also related to other students that he had been counseling several of his gay patients accordingly. The student apparently had several heated discussions with his classmates over the validity and morality of his theory and program. On January 11, 1989, the Interim Policy Administrator wrote to the student informing him that following an investigation of the complaints, there was sufficient evidence to warrant a formal hearing on the charges of sex and sexual orientation harassment. A formal hearing on the charges was held on January 28, 1989.[1] The hearing panel unanimously found that the student was guilty of sexual harassment but refused to convict him of harassment on the basis of sexual orientation. The panel stated:

> In a divided decision the hearing panel finds that the evidence available to the panel indicates that — — — did not harass students on the basis of sexual orientation under the strict definition of "The University of Michigan Policy on Discrimination and Discriminatory Harassment by Students in the University Environment." In accordance with First Amendment rights to free speech and the University's policy of academic freedom, — — — did not violate the policy by discussing either the origins or "curability" of homosexuality in the School of Social Work.

Although the student was not sanctioned over the allegations of sexual orientation harassment, the fact remains that the Policy Administrator—the authoritative voice of the University on these matters—saw no First Amendment problem in forcing the student to a hearing to answer for allegedly harassing statements made in the course of academic discussion and research. Moreover, there is no indication that had the hearing panel convicted rather than acquitted the student, the University would have interceded to protect the interests of academic freedom and freedom of speech.

A second case, which was informally resolved, also demonstrated that the University did not exempt statements made in the course of classroom academic discussions from the sanctions of the policy. On September 28, 1988, a complaint was filed against a student in an entrepreneurship class in the School of Business Administration for reading an allegedly homophobic limerick during a scheduled class public-speaking exercise which ridiculed a well known athlete for his presumed sexual orientation. Complaint No. 88-9-05. The Policy Administrator was able to persuade the perpetrator to attend an educational "gay rap" session, write a letter of apology to the Michigan Daily, and apologize to his class and the matter was dropped. No discussion of the possibility that the limerick was protected speech appears in the file or in the Administrator's notes.

A third incident involved a comment made in the orientation session of a preclinical dentistry class. The class was widely regarded as one of the most difficult for second year dentistry students. To allay fears and concerns at the outset, the class was broken up into small sections to informally discuss anticipated problems. During the ensuing discussion, a student stated that "he had heard that minorities had a difficult time in the course and that he had heard that they were not treated fairly." Complaint No. 88-9-07. A minority professor teaching the class filed a complaint on the grounds that the comment was unfair and hurt her chances for tenure. Following the filing of the complaint, the student was "counseled" about the existence of the policy and agreed to write a letter apologizing for making the comment without adequately verifying the allegation, which he said he had heard from his roommate, a black former dentistry student.[2]

The manner in which these three complaints were handled demonstrated that the University considered serious comments made in the context of classroom discussion to be sanctionable under the Policy. The innocent intent of the speaker was apparently immaterial to whether a complaint would be pursued. Moreover, the Administrator generally failed to consider whether a comment was protected by the First Amendment before informing the accused student that a complaint had been filed. The Administrator instead attempted to persuade the accused student to accept "voluntary" sanctions. Behind this persuasion was, of course, the subtle threat that failure to accept such sanctions might result in a formal hearing. There is no evidence in the record that the Administrator ever declined to pursue a complaint through attempted mediation because the alleged harassing conduct was protected by the First Amendment. Nor is there evidence that the Administrator ever informed an accused harasser during mediation negotiations that the complained of conduct might be protected. The Administrator's manner of enforcing the Policy was constitutionally indistinguishable from a full blown prosecution. The University could not seriously argue that the policy was never interpreted to reach protected conduct. It is clear that the policy was overbroad both on its face and as applied.

C. Vagueness

Doe also urges that the policy be struck down on the grounds that it is impermissibly vague. A statute is unconstitutionally vague when "men of common intelligence must necessarily guess at its meaning." [Citation] A statute must give adequate warning of the conduct which is to be prohibited and must set out explicit standards for those who apply it. "No one may be required at the peril of life, liberty or property to speculate as to the meaning of penal statutes. All are entitled to be informed as to what the State commands or forbids." [Citation] These considerations apply with particular force where the challenged statute acts to inhibit freedoms affirmatively protected by the constitution.
***
[5] Looking at the plain language of the Policy, it was simply impossible to discern any limitation on its scope or any conceptual distinction between protected and unprotected conduct. The structure of the Policy was in two parts; one relates to cause and the other to effect. Both cause and effect must be present to state a prima facie violation of the Policy. The operative words in the cause section required that language must "stigmatize" or "victimize" an individual. However, both of these terms are general and elude precise definition. Moreover, it is clear that the fact that a statement may victimize or stigmatize an individual does not, in and of itself, strip it of protection under the accepted First Amendment tests.

The first of the "effects clauses" stated that in order to be sanctionable, the stigmatizing and victimizing statements had to "involve an express or implied threat to an individual's academic efforts, employment, participation in University sponsored extra-curricular activities or personal safety." It is not clear what kind of conduct would constitute a "threat" to an individual's academic efforts. It might refer to an unspecified threat of future retaliation by the speaker. Or it might equally plausibly refer to the threat to a victim's academic success because the stigmatizing and victimizing speech is so inherently distracting. Certainly the former would be unprotected speech. However, it is not clear whether the latter would.

Moving to the second "effect clause," a stigmatizing or victimizing comment is sanctionable if it has the purpose or reasonably foreseeable effect of interfering with an individual's academic efforts, etc. Again, the question is what conduct will be held to "interfere" with an individual's academic efforts. The language of the policy alone gives no inherent guidance. The one interpretive resource the University provided was withdrawn as "inaccurate," an implicit admission that even the University itself was unsure of the precise scope and meaning of the Policy.

During the oral argument, the Court asked the University's counsel how he would distinguish between speech which was merely offensive, which he conceded was protected, and speech which "stigmatizes or victimizes" on the basis of an invidious factor. Counsel replied "very carefully." The response, while refreshingly candid, illustrated the plain fact that the University never articulated any principled way to distinguish sanctionable from protected speech. Students of common understanding were necessarily forced to guess at whether a comment about a controversial issue would later be found to be sanctionable under the Policy. The terms of the Policy were so vague that its enforcement would violate the due process clause. [Citation]

VI. CONCLUSION

***

While the Court is sympathetic to the University's obligation to ensure equal educational opportunities for all of its students, such efforts must not be at the expense of free speech. Unfortunately, this was precisely what the University did. From the Acting President's December 14 memorandum forward to the adoption of the Policy and continuing through the August 25 hearing, there is no evidence in the record that any officials at the University ever seriously attempted to reconcile their efforts to combat discrimination with the requirements of the First Amendment. The apparent willingness to dilute the values of free speech is ironic in light of the University's previous statements of policy on this matter. In 1977, the Regents adopted the "Statement on Freedom of Speech and Artistic Expression: The Rights and Obligations of Speakers, Performers, Audience Members, and Protesters at the University of Michigan" (Statement) which "reaffirm[ed] formally [the University's] deep and lasting commitment to freedom of speech and artistic expression." The Statement provides in part that

> freedom of speech must not ordinarily be restricted, governed or curtailed in any way by content except where the law, as interpreted by the Supreme Court of Michigan or the Supreme Court of the United States, holds that such an expression does not fall within constitutionally protected free speech. In all instances, the University authorities should act with maximum constraint, even in the face of obvious bad taste or provocation. The belief that some opinion is pernicious, false, or in any other way detestable cannot be grounds for its suppression.

Needless to say, the philosophy expressed in the Statement is diametrically opposed to that reflected in the Acting President's December 14 Memorandum. Apparently, no one involved in the drafting process noted the apparent inconsistency with the Regents' views as expressed in the Statement.

Throughout the case, the University's counsel strenuously urged that First Amendment concerns held a top priority in the development and administration of the Policy. Counsel repeatedly argued that the University interpreted the Policy to reach conduct such as racial slurs and epithets in the classroom directed at an individual victim. However, as the Court observed in its August 25, 1989 bench opinion, what we have heard here this morning . . . from University counsel is a revisionist view of the Policy on Discrimination and Discriminatory Harassment by Students in the University Environment, and it is a view and interpretation of the Policy that was not in the minds of the legislators when it was adopted. And there is nothing in the record that has been presented to the Court which suggests that this was an appropriate interpretation of the policy.

Not only has the administrative enforcement of the Policy been wholly inconsistent with counsel's interpretation, but withdrawal of the Guide, see supra at 13, and the eleventh hour suspension of section 1(c), see supra at 8, suggests that the University had no idea what the limits of the Policy were and it was essentially making up the rules as it went along.
***

ADDENDUM

Inexplicably the Court did not become aware of a conference on legal story telling at the University's Law School in April 1989 until after its Opinion was docketed. Important for consideration of a broader perspective of the issues put by the Policy and the Court's holding of unconstitutionality under the First Amendment is a paper delivered at the conference by Mari J. Matsuda, an associate professor of law at the William S. Richardson School of Law at the University of Hawaii: Public Response To Racist Speech: Considering the Victim's Story, 87 Mich.L.Rev. 2320, August 1989.[3] Professor Matsuda's description of her purpose amply describes the significance of the paper:

This Article attempts to begin a conversation about the first amendment that acknowledges both the civil libertarian's fear of tyranny and the victims' experience of loss of liberty in a society that tolerates racist speech. It suggests criminalization of a narrow, explicitly defined class of racist hate speech, to provide public redress for the most serious harm, while leaving many forms of racist speech to private remedies. . . . This is not an easy legal or moral puzzle, but it is precisely in these places where we feel conflicting tugs at heart and mind that we have the most work to do and the most knowledge to gain.

NOTES

1. The letter stated in part:

> One type of complaint alleges that you have engaged in discrimination and/or discriminatory harassment on the basis of sexual orientation. Specifically the complaints allege the following:
>
> 1. You have made harassing statements in class and in classroom buildings to other students and/or faculty that are intimidating, hostile, and demeaning on the basis of sexual orientation. Specifically — — — complains that you have stated repeatedly that homosexuality is an illness that needs to be "cured".

2. You have made several anti-gay comments to other students, specifically to — — — stating that homosexuality is abnormal and unnatural.

Although the Policy required identification of the complainants, these names were withheld from the Court to protect their privacy.

2. Only a single complaint involving allegedly harassing remarks made in the context of a classroom discussion was dismissed because of First Amendment concerns. A complaint of anti-semitic harassment was filed on March 27, 1989, by a Jewish student in a class on the Holocaust who was offended by another student's suggestion that Jews cynically used the Holocaust to justify Israel's policies toward the Palestinians. Complaint No. 89-3-2. Accordingly to the Administrator's notes, the perpetrator refused to apologize for the comment. The Administrator phoned the complainant and informed her that the comment was protected speech, not covered by the policy.

3. The Opinion was signed and filed around noon on September 22, 1989. The August 1989 issue of the Law Review, while delivered by mail to chambers that morning, was not first read by the Court until that evening. An earlier awareness of Professor Matsuda's paper certainly would have sharpened the Court's view of the issues.

Appendix B

Speech and Speech Acts

"Congress shall make no law . . . abridging the freedom of speech, or of the press. . . ."

—First Amendment, U.S. Constitution

What is "speech"? I'm glad you didn't ask me. Speech seems to be one of those things that one knows what it is until asked to give a definition, as St. Augustine said about time. But some conception of what speech is seems important in this context. For it is widely accepted that even if some speech may be abridged or may be denied full constitutional protection (e.g., threats, fighting words, agreements to commit a crime, etc.), conduct is more subject to legal restriction. The line that divides speech from conduct, however, is quite sticky because *speaking* is a form of conduct. Still, the speech-conduct or expression-action distinction is central to some accounts of the First Amendment, for instance that of Thomas Emerson in his important book *The System of Freedom of Expression*. The distinction between expression and action, he says, provides "the central idea of a system of freedom of expression. . . . A system of freedom of expression cannot exist effectively on any other foundation. . . ."[1] Unfortunately, Emerson gives little explicit guidance on what the "essential qualities" of expression and action are.

The problem of the speech-conduct distinction is compounded by the recognition, if not always the absolute constitutional protection, of such categories as "symbolic speech," and "expressive conduct."[2] All sorts of "speech without words" (pieces of sculpture and music, topless dancing, sleeping in a public park to draw attention to the problem of homelessness) have been claimed to have, and sometimes are granted to have, status under the First Amendment. It seems, then, that there is speech and there is speech, and certain kinds of speech (terrorist threats, for instance) do not, and should not, receive protection under the Constitution. What is the intuition that underlies the distinction between these different kinds of speech?

The question is too large for full treatment here but what we can do is briefly examine some philosophical arguments that have been used to support the claim that pornography and some campus hate speech have a special character that puts them into the unprotected category. These arguments use the notion of "speech acts," which derives from the Oxford philosopher J. L. Austin, whose ground-breaking book is entitled *How to Do Things with Words*.[3]

Before we turn to Austin and the arguments based on his work, it is useful to take note of Catharine A. MacKinnon's lively book *Only Words*. She argues that pornography should not be construed as First Amendment "speech" and should not be given constitutional protection, as courts have done. "Law's proper concern here," she says, "is not what speech says, but with what it does." And what it *does* is subordinate women through sex. MacKinnon writes:

> I am not saying that pornography is conduct and therefore not speech, or that it does things and therefore says nothing and is without meaning. . . . At a certain point, when those who are hurt by them become real, some words are recognized as the acts that they are. . . . It is not new to observe that while the doctrinal distinction between speech and action is on one level obvious, on another level it makes little sense. In social inequality, it makes almost none.[4]

Now, what we are interested in is the idea, as MacKinnon puts it, that some words should be recognized "as the acts that they are." We cannot further explore the speech-conduct problem as an issue in constitutional law.

The question of how things are done with words goes back to the early part of this century, at least. The Scandinavian legal theorist Axel Hägerström wondered about this phenomenon in connection with Roman law. In this system the recitation of certain verbal formulas is necessary in order to effectuate various changes in legal relations (e.g., in the transfer of rights). Hägerström thought the phenomenon depended on the survival of a primitive belief in word magic, in the way that the magician's formula "abracadabra" is supposed to make things happen in the real world.[5] Later, in the 1930s, the English philosopher H. A. Prichard exchanged correspondence with Austin on promising. Prichard's perplexity was: How could it be that saying something ("I promise") creates an obligation? He had no solution, but the exchange apparently stimulated in Austin the idea that to say "I promise" is not just to say something but to do something, and so too for other utterances.[6] Here is a brief account of Austin's approach.

Austin began by noting that some ordinary language sentences are not primarily used to state facts, to make true or false statements, but rather to do something, for instance, christening (or giving a name), promising, and urging:

I christen this ship the *Queen Elizabeth.*
I promise to come tomorrow.
I urge you to stop smoking.

Such sentences he called *performatives*, which he contrasted with *constantives*, basically fact-stating statements. A performative can go wrong, "misfire," bc "unhappy" as he put it, be infelicitous. Naming a ship, for example, will not be successful unless certain institutional arrangements are in place. More generally, a performative may fail unless certain *felicity conditions* are satisfied, of which conditions only two will be mentioned here: (1) There must be a conventional procedure having a conventional effect, and the circumstances and persons must be appropriate, as specified by the procedure; and (2) the procedure must be executed correctly and completely.[7] Thus, my attempt to name your child Murgatroyd will not succeed because I am not the appropriate person to give it a name.

For various reasons Austin came to find the performative-constantive distinction unsatisfactory, and he moved on to the idea that utterances perform specific actions, do things, through having specific *forces*. In doing something by saying something, three kinds of act are performed:

1. *Locutionary act:* the utterance of a sentence with determinate sense and reference;
2. *Illocutionary act:* the making of a statement, an offer, a promise, etc., in uttering a sentence, by virtue of the conventional *force* associated with it;
3. *Perlocutionary act:* the bringing about of effects on the audience by means of uttering the sentence.

Thus, to use Austin's example, in performing the locutionary act of saying "Shoot her!" the utterance, in appropriate circumstances, will variously have the illocutionary force of ordering, urging, or advising the addressee to shoot someone, and the perlocutionary effect of persuading, forcing, or frightening the addressee into shooting her. Roughly, the illocutionary act is performed *in* saying something, and the perlocutionary act is performed *by* saying something. Austin's main interest is the illocutionary act, to which the term *speech act* is particularly attached.[8]

In a very stimulating article, Rae Langton wants to defend, or at least make plausible, MacKinnon's view that pornography not only depicts the subordination of women, not only causes the subordination of women, but also *is*, in and of itself, a form of subordination: pornography is an *illocutionary act* of subordination.[9] (Langton, however, is not concerned to argue that pornography should be censored; she leaves that issue aside.)

Dr. Langton compares pornography and various speech acts in South Africa under the apartheid regime. The legislator's utterance "Blacks are not permitted to vote" is an illocutionary act of subordination. For such an utterance unfairly ranks blacks as having inferior worth, legitimates discriminatory behavior on the part of whites, and unjustly deprives blacks of some important powers. Similarly, pornography—aside from the harm to women that it causes—ranks women as sex objects; it represents degrading and abusive sexual behavior in such a way as to endorse the degradation. MacKinnon, she says, has a striking list of illocutionary verbs: "Pornography sexualizes rape, battery, sexual harassment . . . and child abuse; it . . . *celebrates*, *promotes*, *authorizes*, and *legitimates* them."[10]

Now, as Langton notes, just as in the legislator's speech act under apartheid, for pornography to have the character of an illocutionary act of subordination, it must satisfy a certain felicity condition: the *authoritative* position of the speaker in the relevant domain. The authority is necessary in order for the locutions to count as illocutionary acts having the force in question. For example, when I say the base runner is "out" but the umpire calls him "safe," it is his call that counts; he has the authority, I don't. Such a call is labeled a *verdictive* by Austin (actions of ranking, valuing). There are also *exercitives* (ordering, permitting, prohibiting, enacting a law), which also depend on the requisite authority. "Pornography is, first, verdictive speech that ranks women as sex objects, and, second, exercitive speech that legitimates sexual violence. Since sexual violence is not simply harm, simply crime, but discriminatory behavior, pornography subordinates because it legitimates this behavior. . . . [P]ornography is an *illocutionary* act of subordination."[11]

Langton offers various qualifications to her approach but comes quickly to the "heart of the controversy." In order to answer the question, "Does pornography subordinate?" she says, one must first answer another: "Do its speakers have authority?"[12]

This latter question, Dr. Langton admits, is an empirical question, which is not something to which philosophy supplies an answer. Yet she does strongly suggest that its speakers do have authority within a certain domain—"the game of sex"— just as the speech of the umpire is authoritative within the domain of baseball. She cites statistics about the attitudes and behavior of (some) males toward sex: the fifty percent of boys who "think it is okay for a man to rape a woman if he is sexually aroused by her," the fifteen percent of male college undergraduates who say they have raped a woman on a date, and so on. *If* these attitudes and behaviors are the result of pornography, the best explanation, Langton suggests, may be that pornography is authoritative for these males and that it is an illocutionary act of subordination.

Granting the validity of these statistics (a rather questionable matter, in my opinion), however, there is no proof offered that these attitudes and behaviors are the result of pornography, though pornography may be an influence in some cases. Assuming that all of the fifteen percent of the male undergraduates are consumers of pornography, does that show that pornography is an authority for their (criminal) sex lives? Does the fact that A influences B, show that A has authority over (or for) B?

More particularly, though, absent from Langton's argument is an analysis of the concept of authority. I rank movies, judge some to be good and others to be bad. Is my judgment a verdictive or isn't it? I don't think I have, or need to have, any authority to issue such judgments. If someone respected my judgment on movies, would that make me an authority for him? Perhaps so, but would that make me an authority in the same sense in which I have the authority to assign grades to students in my courses, which I cannot do for another instructor's courses?

What makes the publisher of *Hustler* an authority in the domain of pornography? Authority is not only relative to a domain, but it is also relative to persons. For *whom* is the publisher an authority? All men? Some men? How many men? In any case, his putative authority is different in kind from the authority that the Commander-in-Chief has over members of the military. Especially if authority can be of different types, we need an analysis of authority before we can answer Langton's empirical question: "Do the speakers of pornography have authority?" and also the question: "Does pornography have the character of an illocutionary act of subordination?"

In a clearly written article, which we shall discuss only briefly, Professor Andrew Altman rejects two standard arguments for campus hate-speech codes: namely, that such regulations are important in fighting racial and sexual subordination in society at large, and that they are needed to provide students with a comfortable learning environment so that all will have a genuinely equal educational opportunity.[13] Moreover, he is rather leery of codes that would, or even could, be overly restrictive of speech. He uses Austin to defend a narrowly tailored hate-speech code, such as Stanford's, which prohibits certain face-to-face slurs and epithets.

Some, but not all, forms of hate speech, says Altman, "involve the performance of a certain species of illocutionary act, i.e., the act of treating someone as a moral subordinate."[14] This kind of act treats a person as though his or her life is inherently less valuable, and his or her interests less important, than the lives and interests of some reference group. Such words as "kike," "faggot," "nigger," and "spic" are typically used for such linguistic acts of subordination; they are the conventional, verbal instruments of subordination. They carry roughly the same social meaning that spitting on someone carries in our culture.

Professor Altman believes it is common ground, in the speech code debate, that universities stand under an obligation to provide their students equal educational opportunities without regard to race, gender, or sexual orientation. Such an obligation mandates adoption of certain policies and it bars the adoption of others. Plainly, Altman states, excluding blacks from the library would be a violation of that obligation. In addition, while certain policies might not be mandated, some are reasonable to adopt as a way of honoring the commitment to equal opportunity. One such reasonable policy is a narrowly tailored hate-speech code that penalizes face-to-face use of the language of subordination. Such a code, Altman thinks, need not pose a problem for the university's commitment to free expression and the interchange of ideas and opinions.

Somewhat like Langton's argument on pornography, then, Altman's argument presents the case for regarding some hate speech as illocutionary acts of subordination, and I think it is deficient on exactly the same issue—authority. Altman, near the beginning of his article, in fact presents the authority of the speaker as one of the felicity conditions for an illocutionary act; without such authority the act will "misfire." But he does not return to it in his discussion of hate speech and does not explain the supposed authority that the speaker has.

How necessary is authority? I may insult you by calling you an "idiot" in public, and I have thereby performed an illocutionary act. But what sort of authority do I have? Do I need authority in order to be rude or demean you? Austin thought that insults had a certain peculiarity. In a discussion of what he called "explicit performatives," he points out that our language does not have the expression "I (hereby) insult you."[15] We don't insult a person merely by saying that. We can compare this to "I (hereby) bequeath my watch to John," stated in a will;

"bequeath" is a performative verb. Austin does not discuss insults any further, but I suppose he would say that the conventions of our language are such that certain locutions constitute insults in particular social contexts, and that no special authority is needed there.

The cases presented by Langton and Altman are different from the above. Pornography *does* demean women and some hate speech *does* demean, or is meant to demean, women and minorities. But Langton and Altman are arguing for something more. They respectively want to establish that pornography and hate speech *subordinate* their targets. And this is why some sort of authority is required. Until, however, we know what this is, their cases must be regarded as inconclusive.

NOTES

1. Thomas I. Emerson, *The System of Freedom of Expression* (New York: Random House, 1970), 17. Emerson's use of the term "expression" rather than the (then) more current term "speech" may have been deliberate, as the former suggests something broader. For a superb analytical treatment of the First Amendment, see William W. Van Alstyne, *Interpretations of the First Amendment* (Durham, N.C.: Duke University Press, 1984).

2. The problem has a parallel in the second religion clause of the First Amendment, which forbids laws prohibiting "the free exercise thereof." Religious belief and opinion were once confidently distinguished by the Supreme Court from conduct. The first major decision on the free exercise clause (*Reynolds v. United States*, 98 U.S. 145 (1879)) upheld a federal law making polygamy illegal as applied to a Mormon whose religious duty was to practice polygamy: "Congress was deprived of all legislative power over mere opinion, but was left free to reach actions which were in violation of social duties or subversive of good order." A religious person, however, could hardly accept the idea that his beliefs were "mere opinion" and thus easily distinguishable from the actions that his beliefs mandate; in fact belief and action may be inseparable. Eventually, the Court became more solicitous of conduct pursuant to religious belief, though it did not recognize all such conduct as an absolute, protected freedom.

3. J. L. Austin, *How to Do Things with Words* (Cambridge, Mass.: Harvard University Press, 1962; 2d ed. 1975).

4. Catharine A. MacKinnon, *Only Words* (Cambridge, Mass.: Harvard University Press, 1993), 29f. "Austin," says MacKinnon, "is less an authority for my particular development of 'doing things with words' and more of a foundational exploration of the view in language theory that some speech can be action" (*Only Words*, n. 31 to chapter 1). A detailed accounting of crimes that have not been questioned from the perspective of free speech is given in Kent Greenawalt, *Speech, Crime, and the Uses of Language* (Oxford: Oxford University Press, 1989). The intuitions that underlie this categorization turn on the "situation altering" character of the utterances, a notion that Greenawalt finds more useful here than Austin's ideas of performative utterances and illocutionary forces.

5. See the editor's introduction to Axel Hägerström, *Inquiries into the Nature of Law and Morals*, ed. K. Olivecrona, trans. C. D. Broad (Stockholm: Almqvist & Wiksell, 1953).

6. See G. J. Warnock, *J. L. Austin* (London and New York: Routledge, 1989), 105. For a concise exposition of Austin, see Stephen C. Levinson, *Pragmatics* (Cambridge: Cambridge University Press, 1983), 226–38.

7. The full statement is given in *How to Do Things with Words* (2d ed.), 14f. Sometimes the speaker will need to secure "uptake," an appropriate response from the hearer: "I bet you a dollar it will rain tomorrow." "You're on." And usually the speaker will have to have an intention to perform an illocution of a certain kind. Even though Austin came to find the performative-constantive distinction unsatisfactory, the notion of felicity conditions remained important.

8. The word "force," it might be objected, is metaphorical and one may wonder whether it has a literal translation. Axel Hägerström apparently thought that only fact-stating language is meaningful and that the belief in the effectiveness of the Roman legal formulas therefore must have rested on a belief in something like a magical power. Austin's point, on the other hand, rather is that the performative nature of some utterances is as much a function of language use as the fact-stating function.

9. Rae Langton, "Speech Acts and Unspeakable Acts," 22 *Philosophy and Public Affairs* (1993), 293–330. Part of Langton's article is devoted to establishing the plausibility of the claim that pornography "silences" women in a way that constitutes illocutionary disablement. We are not concerned with this part of her argument.

10. Langton, 307 (emphasis in original), quoting MacKinnon.

11. Langton, 307f.

12. Langton, 311.

13. Andrew Altman, "Speech Acts and Hate Speech," in *An Ethical Education*, ed. M. N. S. Sellers (Oxford/Providence: Berg Publishers, 1994), 127–141.

14. Altman, 130. Such acts, Altman carefully argues, must be distinguished from assertions or justifications (pseudo-scientific, theological, etc.) of the moral inferiority of a group.

15. *How to Do Things with Words* (2d ed.), 68. Of course, one can say " I was insulted."

Index

vagueness and overbreadth, 100–104
Van Alstyne, Professor William, 80
verbal harassment, 49, 83–86
Volokh, Professor Eugene, 88

Wagstaff, Professor (Groucho Marx), 18
Walker, Samuel, 47

"water buffalo" affair, 61
Weinreich, Max, 40, 42
Wilson, E. O., 38
Words That Wound, 50, 55

Zionism, 72

About the Author

Martin P. Golding received his undergraduate education at the University of California at Los Angeles and took his doctorate at Columbia University, where he taught until 1970. He then went to John Jay College of Criminal Justice for six years, after which he joined the philosophy department at Duke University. He served as chairman of the department from 1976 until 1986. Professor Golding directs the joint law-philosophy program, and currently is professor of philosophy and professor of law at Duke. He has held a number of visiting positions, including one in the faculty of law at Bar-Ilan University in Israel. In 1985, he was a senior Fulbright lecturer in Australia. He has held fellowships from the National Endowment for the Humanities and the National Humanities Center. From 1969 to 1989 he was the secretary-treasurer of the American Society for Political and Legal Philosophy. Professor Golding is the author of *Philosophy of Law*, which has been translated into Japanese and Chinese, and *Legal Reasoning;* he is editor of *Jewish Law and Legal Theory*. He has also published articles and chapters of books, including a number of papers on the concept of rights and papers on the rule of law. Professor Golding's teaching interests include courses in philosophy of law, responsibility in law and morals, ethics, and Jewish law.